QUILTS *from the* SMITHSONIAN

12 Designs Inspired by the Textile Collection of the National Museum of American History

Mimi Dietrich

That Patchwork Place®

DEDICATION

This book is dedicated to today's quilters. We've come a long way and have created wonderful quilts. Most of our quilts are not in museums; they are loved by our families and friends.

ACKNOWLEDGMENTS

This project is the result of the ideas, dreams, work, and stitches of many devoted quilt lovers. It is with great pleasure that I would like to thank:

Nancy Martin, president of That Patchwork Place, for having faith in me;

Barbara Weiland, Marion Shelton, and Alane Redon, who make it a pleasure to work with That Patchwork Place;

The Office of Product Development and Licensing, Smithsonian Institution;

The Custodian of the Quilt Collection, National Museum of American History;

Rick Cohan, President of RJR Fashion Fabrics, and Demetria Zahoudanis, Director of Marketing, for providing wonderful fabrics and textile documentation;

Laurie Scott, who researched information about quilt names and pieced the Plaid Patch quilt;

Norma Campbell, who provided enthusiasm for the project and pieced the Scrap Baskets quilt;

"The Rosebuds of the Chesapeake," who appliquéd the Chesapeake Rose quilt during the summer of '94;

"The Catonsville Quilt and Tea Society," whose members appliquéd and pieced the All-American Eagle quilt during our Friday morning meetings;

Pat Brousil, who beautifully hand pieced the Chips and Whetstones quilt;

Eleanor Eckman, who appliquéd the Spring Tulips quilt in a winter month;

Mary Hickey, who sewed thousands of Pinwheels;

Kay Twit, who used her beloved vintage fabric for the Wild Fabric Chase quilt;

Julie Powell of Vintage Textiles and Tools, who helped Kay Twit find fabrics representative of the period;

Jennifer Goldsborough and Karen Ringrose, for their lessons in museum etiquette;

Georgina B. Fries Quilting Service, Bellwether Dry Goods, Lothian, MD 20711;

Betty Kiser, for saying magic words;

Gail Binney-Stiles, for sharing her quote, "Take a quilt from the past . . . " which appears on page 5;

Bob, Jon, and Ryan Dietrich for living this experience with me;

And, most of all, thanks to all of my talented friends and students who stitched new heirlooms for the future.

CREDITS

Editor-in-Chief/Technical Editor . . . . Barbara Weiland
Managing Editor . . . . Greg Sharp
Copy Editor . . . . Liz McGehee
Proofreader . . . . Leslie Phillips
Design Director . . . . Judy Petry
Text and Cover Designer . . . . Kay Green
Production Assistant . . . . Shean Bemis
Illustrator . . . . Laurel Strand
Illustration Assistants . . . . Lisa McKenney
Carolyn Kraft
Photographer . . . . Brent Kane
Photography Assistant . . . . Richard Lipshay

Quilts from the Smithsonian: 12 Designs Inspired by the Textile Collection of the National Museum of American History
©1995 Smithsonian Institution

That Patchwork Place, Inc.
PO Box 118
Bothell, WA 98041-0118
USA

Printed in the United States of America
00 99 98 97 96 95   6 5 4 3 2 1

Mission Statement

WE ARE DEDICATED TO PROVIDING QUALITY PRODUCTS THAT ENCOURAGE CREATIVITY AND PROMOTE SELF-ESTEEM IN OUR CUSTOMERS AND OUR EMPLOYEES.

WE STRIVE TO MAKE A DIFFERENCE IN THE LIVES WE TOUCH.

That Patchwork Place is an employee-owned, financially secure company.

Library of Congress Cataloging–in–Publication Data
Smithsonian Institution.
Quilts from the Smithsonian : 12 designs inspired by the textile collection of the National Museum of American History / Mimi Dietrich.
p.   cm.
ISBN 1–56477–120–2
1. Patchwork—Patterns. 2. Quilting—Patterns. 3. Appliqué—Patterns. I. Dietrich, Mimi. II. National Museum of American History (U.S.) III. Title.
TT835.S59 1995
746.46'041—dc20   95–20465
                                                                              CIP

That Patchwork Place is a licensee of the Smithsonian Institution.

TABLE OF CONTENTS

INTRODUCTION 4

THE SMITHSONIAN INSTITUTION 6

THE SMITHSONIAN QUILT
FABRIC COLLECTION 7

THE QUILTS..................... 8
Plaid Patch 8
Wild Fabric Chase 13
Sunflower Garden 18
Carpenter's Wheel 24
Scrap Baskets 29
Chips and Whetstones 34
Spring Tulips 40
All-American Eagle 45
Chesapeake Rose 52
Welcome Pineapple 58
Lilies of the Quilters 64
Pinwheels 70

QUILTMAKING BASICS FOR
PATCHWORK AND APPLIQUÉ 77
Fabric Selection and Preparation.......... 77
Tools and Supplies 78
Patchwork Basics 80
    Hand Piecing 80
    Machine Piecing................... 82
Appliqué 83
    Traditional Hand Appliqué............ 83
    Freezer-Paper Appliqué 87
Assembly and Finishing Techniques 88
    Squaring Up Blocks 88
    Setting the Blocks Together 89
    Adding Borders.................... 89
    Marking the Quilting Design.......... 91
    Layering and Basting 91
    Quilting......................... 92
    Binding 93
    Adding a Label.................... 94

INTRODUCTION

Many quiltmakers are inspired by quilts made in the past. Perhaps they slept under a quilt made long ago by a family member. Perhaps they saw antique quilts at a show or admired an exhibit of vintage quilts in a museum. These wonderful old quilts provide us with a tangible piece of history. This fascination with history motivates us to re-create our American heritage with our own stitches.

As we make quilts, we draw inspiration from historical designs, and we stand in awe of museum quilts. Many of us dream that our quilts will survive to touch and inspire quilters of the future. Some of us even have secret dreams that one quilt we make will be treasured and conserved in a museum setting.

I feel very privileged to have had the opportunity to work on this book of projects inspired by quilts in the collection of the Smithsonian Institution's National Museum of American History. Each time I visited the textile collection in the museum, my heart skipped a beat and I pinched myself to make sure this was really happening to me. I saw quilts by appointment only and viewed a small number each time. Each quilt was carefully removed from storage and gently unwrapped to reveal a quilted masterpiece. Some of the quilts were extremely fragile. Others were as bright and fresh as if they were new. Each one took my breath away. Each quilt had its own special appeal, whether it be skillful appliqué, tiny hand-pieced patches, or the most luscious quilting stitches I have ever seen. It was a fabulous experience.

To begin the project, before actually seeing the quilts, I looked at slides and black-and-white photographs of the quilts in the collection. I chose the quilts in this book for their designs, because they reflect a variety of quilting techniques. Six of the new quilt designs are patchwork, ranging from a simple Ninepatch to the more complicated Chips and Whetstones. Three

of the quilts are appliquéd: the Chesapeake Rose is a full-size quilt and the Spring Tulips and Welcome Pineapple are wonderful wall hangings. Three of the quilts combine patchwork and appliqué methods. I chose these quilts for quilters who like a variety of techniques.

I began this project thinking that I would write directions and produce the quilts exactly like the old ones. I changed my mind with the first quilt I made. The "Sunflower Garden" quilt, shown on page 19, was inspired by the old quilt, but I wanted so to make it with one of the bright sunflower prints available in my local quilt shop. I also realized I didn't have the time to hand piece twenty Sunflower blocks and still work on the other quilts. So the "Sunflower Garden" grew out of the old Sunflower quilt; it's different from the original quilt, and I had a wonderful time making it!

Then I started to make the second quilt, "Plaid Patch," just like the old quilt. The official measurements for the old quilt list the block measurement as 5 1/2". In order to make the directions easier to use, especially for rotary-cutting techniques, I rounded the measurement to 6". Then the fabric search began. With the abundance of plaids available in several shops, I was sure I would find the "perfect" fabrics. I was surprised and disappointed, but changed my search and pursued fabrics with the "feel" of the old quilt. The new quilt is not exactly the same as the Smithsonian quilt, but I love it! In the process of making the quilts for this book, I learned a few things about reproducing the past, and this book became a book of quilts *inspired* by the Smithsonian quilts.

It was a fun challenge to design the patterns in this book. I used everything I've learned about pattern drafting since I saw Jinny Beyer draw a Ninepatch in 1979. I drafted the patchwork patterns on graph paper, using the original measurements of the old quilts. Some measurements were provided by the curatorial staff of the textile collection; others were taken by actually measuring the quilts. Some sizes quoted for the old quilts may seem inaccurate, especially for quilts that are square. Many old quilts have unusually sized blocks. When different blocks are measured on a quilt, there may be a discrepancy in size. This occurs because measurements are taken now, long after the quilt was made. Blocks shrink from the quilting process, from laundering, or simply from use. Some of the new quilts were adapted, using sizes more appropriate for cutting and sewing. For example, the new Lily blocks measure 8" instead of 8¼", and the Sunflower block has sixteen petals instead of nineteen. Since some of the old quilts are very large, I decided to make most of the new quilts in this book smaller so they could be used as wall hangings.

To make the patterns for the appliqué designs, I used photographs of the old quilts. I enlarged the photograph with a photocopy machine until the image blurred. Then, I traced the design neatly with a fine-line pen and continued to photocopy until the design was the correct size. I traced symmetrical designs by folding tracing paper in half. I used a proportional scale to ensure correct sizes on the enlargements.

If you are new to quiltmaking or need information on quilt assembly and finishing techniques, you may want to read the section entitled "Quiltmaking Basics for Patchwork and Appliqué," beginning on page 77. There you will find information on fabric selection, cutting and piecing methods, appliqué, and everything you need to know to assemble and finish your quilt.

Admire the old quilts, use the patterns included in this book, but make a quilt that has your own personal touch. Use new fabrics to make an updated version of a quilt, use fabric adapted from older fabric to give your new quilt the "feel" of the old quilt, or search for vintage fabrics to make your quilt authentic. Add your personality and individual creativity to your quilt.

Please don't copy the old quilts exactly. These masterpiece quilts are conserved in the museum because they are representative of quilting techniques and specific periods in history. I can't imagine trying to reproduce the quilting in the Rose of Sharon quilt shown on page 52. Have fun with these patterns, be inspired by their designs, and make a quilt today that will be great in the future!

"Take a quilt from the past
add the present
make a quilt for the future."

THE SMITHSONIAN INSTITUTION

Smithsonian Institution Building (the Castle), south view and the Enid A. Haupt Garden

The Smithsonian Institution in Washington, D. C., was created in 1846 by an act of Congress. James Smithson, a prominent British scientist, willed his entire estate to the United States of America "to found at Washington, under the name of the Smithsonian Institution, an establishment for the increase and diffusion of knowledge . . ."

The Smithsonian Institution is the largest complex of museums in the world. It consists of museums and galleries, including the National Museum of American History, which houses the extensive quilt collection. In the textile collection there are more than three hundred quilts in a range of sizes and patterns. The collection also includes other items such as quilt squares, coverlets, shawls, baskets, tablecloths, laces, and framed needlework. The national quilt collection began in the 1890s when John Brenton Copp of Stonington, Connecticut, donated three late-eighteenth- and early-nineteenth-century quilts to the Smithsonian.

THE SMITHSONIAN QUILT FABRIC COLLECTION

In 1994, the Smithsonian Institution awarded RJR Fashion Fabrics a license to produce fabrics selected from material found in nineteenth-century quilts housed in the National Museum of American History. They selected the Rising Sun quilt made by Mary Betsy Totten as the theme of their first collection. Eleven different patterns were printed and adapted from five beautiful nineteenth-century quilts. The designs ranged from large floral motifs to small calico prints. The patterns were available in three color groups, which could be mixed, matched, and blended with each other. One grouping offered the same colors of the Rising Sun quilt; the additional colors were representative of the period as approved by the curatorial staff of the textile collection, National Museum of American History, Smithsonian Institution.

RJR Fabrics plans additional fabric collections based on the quilt collection at the Smithsonian. All of the cotton fabrics are printed in the United States. The printing technique used is an engraved roller process, a technique used in the United States since 1825. The machines used in this process enable RJR to produce, as closely as possible, the intricacy of the nineteenth-century designs.

We are fortunate to have these innovative fabrics available to inspire a traditional feeling in our modern quilts. I have used fabrics from the first RJR collection in two of the quilt projects in this book: "Chips and Whetstones" on page 35 and "Welcome Pineapple" on page 59. Fabrics from the second collection are shown in the photo below.

PLAID PATCH

Quilt Dimensions: 77" x 94" ❧ Block Size: 6" x 6"

*T*he Smithsonian Institution's National Museum of American History has many Ninepatch quilts in its collection. This is my favorite. The colors are vibrant, the plaids are cozy, and the red plaid triangles set around the border create a contemporary appearance. Not much is known about this wonderful old quilt, only that it was made in the third quarter of the nineteenth century.

The original quilt was made with wool, wool-cotton, and cotton fabrics. The new quilt was made with cotton solids, prints, and plaids that look similar to the old fabrics and maintain the "feel" of the vintage quilt. It was fun to search for the "perfect" plaid fabrics.

The Ninepatch design is one of the simplest and most versatile patchwork patterns. The seams are straight and easy to match, but there are many design possibilities. Most Ninepatch designs consist of nine equally sized units in the block. This design variation, with small corner squares, is often referred to as "Puss in the Corner." The squares are set "on point," with setting triangles along the edges of the quilt.

Each piece of the nineteenth-century quilt was probably cut using a template and scissors. As we approach the twenty-first century, we have rotary-cutting tools and techniques that make quiltmaking fast and fun. For comparison, I am including directions for making this quilt using both traditional and contemporary methods.

NINEPATCH
*quilt from the
Smithsonian collection,
182.9cm x 226.7cm
(72¹/₄"x 89¹/₄").*

PLAID PATCH
by Laurie Scott and Mimi Dietrich, 1994, Baltimore,
Maryland, 77" x 94". Quilted by Amish friends.

MATERIALS: 44"-WIDE FABRIC

1¼ yds. light plaid for
small corner squares

2¼ yds. bright blue for rectangles

1¼ yds. bright red for center squares

3¾ yds. denim blue for setting squares
and binding

1¼ yds. red plaid for setting triangles

5½ yds. coordinating fabric for backing

81" x 98" piece of batting

Thread

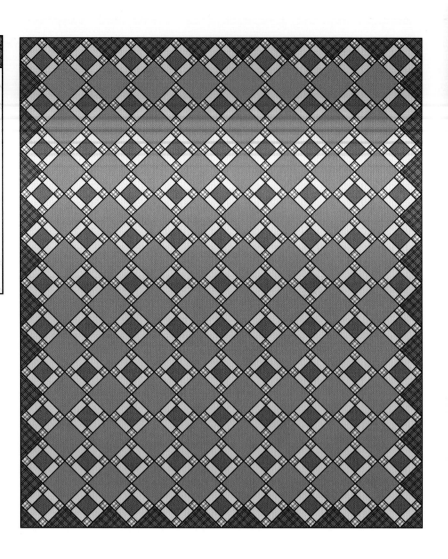

Puss in the Corner　　　　Setting Block

Template Cutting

Use the templates on pages 95–96.
From the light plaid fabric, cut:
396 Template #1

From the bright blue fabric, cut:
396 Template #2

From the bright red fabric, cut:
99 Template #3

From the denim blue fabric, cut:
80 Template #4

From the red plaid fabric, cut:
36 Template #5

4 Template #6

Traditional Block Assembly

1. Sew 2 light plaid squares (Template #1) to the short ends of each bright blue rectangle (Template #2). Press the seams toward the rectangle.

2. Sew 2 bright blue rectangles to opposite sides of each bright red square (Template #3). Press the seams toward the rectangles.

3. Sew the units together to make a total of 99 Puss in the Corner blocks. Press.

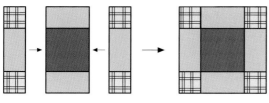

Make 99

4. See "Quilt Top Assembly and Finishing," page 12.

Rotary Cutting

All measurements include ¹/₄″-wide seam allowances. Cut all strips across the fabric width.

From the light plaid fabric, cut:
20 strips, each 2" wide

From the bright blue fabric, cut:
10 strips, each 3¹/₂" wide

18 strips, each 2" wide

From the bright red fabric, cut:
9 strips, each 3¹/₂" wide

From the denim blue fabric, cut:
14 strips, each 6¹/₂" wide. Crosscut the strips at 6¹/₂" intervals to cut a total of 80 alternate setting squares, each 6¹/₂" x 6¹/₂".

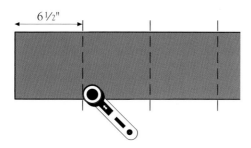

From the red plaid fabric, cut:
18 squares, each 7" x 7". Stack the squares in sets of 2 and cut once diagonally for a total of 36 side setting triangles.*

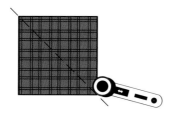

1 square, 7¹/₄" x 7¹/₄". Cut twice diagonally for a total of 4 corner setting triangles.*

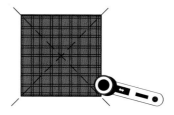

*Normally, side and corner setting triangles are cut so that their long edge is on the straight of grain. This prevents the outer edges of the quilt from stretching as you work. However, since I wanted the plaid to be on the diagonal, I had to break traditional rules. Handle these triangles with care!

Speed-Pieced Block Assembly

1. Sew 2 of the 2"-wide light plaid strips to 1 of the 3¹/₂"-wide bright blue strips as shown. Press the seams toward the bright blue strip. Make a total of 10 of these strip-pieced units. Each of the finished units should measure 6¹/₂" wide. Crosscut a total of 198 segments, each 2" wide, from the strip-pieced units.

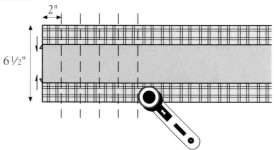

2. Sew 2 of the 2"-wide bright blue strips to 1 of the 3¹/₂"-wide bright red strips as shown. Press the seams toward the bright blue strips. Make a total of 9 of these strip-pieced units. Each of the finished units should measure 6¹/₂" wide. Crosscut a total of 99 segments, each 3¹/₂" wide, from the strip-pieced units.

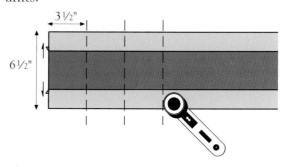

3. Join the segments as shown to make a total of 99 Puss in the Corner blocks.

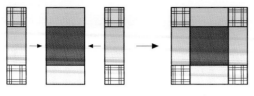

Make 99

Quilt Top Assembly and Finishing

Refer to "Assembly and Finishing Techniques," beginning on page 88.

1. Arrange the pieced blocks, the denim blue alternate setting squares, and the side and corner setting triangles in diagonal rows as shown. Sew the blocks and triangles together in diagonal rows. Press the seams toward the denim blue squares. Sew the rows together, adding the corner triangles last.

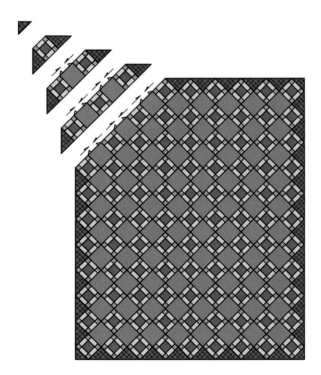

2. Mark the quilting design. The design used on this quilt is a traditional pattern known as "Baptist Fan." Beginning in one corner of the quilt top, draw curved lines 3/4" apart until the fan is 5" wide. Cover the quilt top with the quilting design.

3. Layer the quilt top with batting and backing; baste.
4. Quilt on the marked lines.
5. Bind the edges with denim blue binding.
6. Add a label to your finished quilt. See page 94.

WILD FABRIC CHASE

Quilt Dimensions: 37¼" x 37¼"
Flying Geese Block Size: 12¾" x 12¾"
Setting Block Size: 3¾" x 3¾"

The Wild Goose Chase quilt in the Smithsonian collection was made in the late nineteenth century by Alma Baker Starr of Ridgefield Springs, New York. It was given to the Smithsonian by her granddaughter, Mrs. Leo Rosenbaum. The block design in this quilt is most often referred to as Wild Goose Chase. The Flying Geese triangles represent the formation of geese as they soar through the air. Small Ninepatch blocks were pieced to use as setting squares in the sashing.

The Wild Goose Chase blocks in the original quilt were made with a scrappy combination of geometrics, florals, and polka dots that were roller-printed on cotton; plaids and florals printed on wool-cotton; and florals printed on wool, solid-color wools, pale green silk, and plain white cotton. The quilt represents an extensive collection of late-nineteenth-century fabrics.

My friend Kay Twit collects vintage fabrics. When she saw the photographs of the Smithsonian quilt, she became very excited and pointing to one of the fabrics, exclaimed "I have that fabric! I have that fabric!" Kay decided to make a new wall hanging, studying the photographs to interpret the fabrics and prints in the original quilt as closely as possible. She combined vintage cotton fabrics with new white cotton fabric, giving the old fabrics a fresh sparkle!

Making the wall hanging gave Kay an excuse to shop for special fabrics as she attempted to find fabrics representative of the period. It was truly her "wild fabric chase"! Her hand piecing created neat and tidy patchwork triangles, highlighting each special fabric. She used seventy-nine fabrics to make her wonderful sampler of old fabrics with the definite "feel" of the original quilt, shown at right.

If you collect fabrics, this quilt is your challenge!

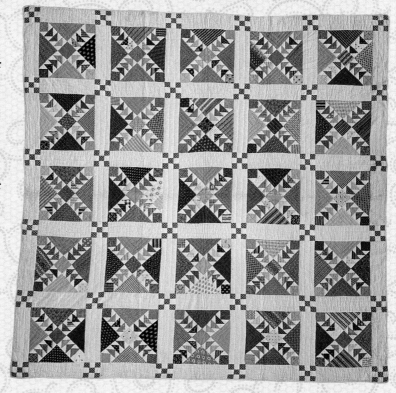

WILD GOOSE CHASE
*quilt from the Smithsonian
collection, 214.3cm x 218.5cm
(84½" x 85⅞").*

2 yds. white for patchwork,
sashing, and binding

1/4 yd. red for Ninepatch
setting squares

Scraps of colorful cottons
for patchwork triangles

1 1/4 yds. coordinating fabric
for backing

40" x 40" piece of batting

Thread

Flying Geese

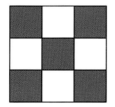

Ninepatch
Setting Block

Cutting

*Use the templates on page 97. Cutting information
for one block and for the wall hanging is given on
each template. If you wish to make a large quilt like
the original, make 25 scrappy Flying Geese blocks
and 36 red-and-white Ninepatch blocks.*

From the white fabric, cut:

12 strips, each 4 1/4" x 13 1/4", for the sashing

36 Template #1 for the Ninepatch setting blocks.
If you prefer, you can rotary-cut 2 strips, each
1 3/4" x 42", from the white fabric. Cut a total of
36 squares, each 1 3/4" x 1 3/4", from the strips.

128 Template #2 for the Flying Geese blocks

From the red fabric, cut:

45 Template #1 for the Ninepatch setting blocks.
If you prefer, you can rotary-cut 2 strips, each
1 3/4" x 42", from the red fabric. Cut a total of
45 squares, each 1 3/4" x 1 3/4", from the strips.

From the scraps, cut:

48 Template #3 for the Flying Geese

16 Template #4 for the block corners

4 Template #5 for the block centers

16 Template #6 for the block side triangles

Flying Geese Block Assembly

1. Sew 2 small white triangles (Template #2) to each
medium corner square (Template #4) as shown.
Press the seams toward the square in each of the
resulting corner units.

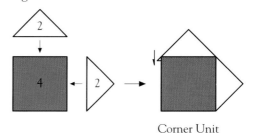

Corner Unit
Make 16

2. Sew 2 white triangles (Template #2) to each of the scrappy triangles (Template #3). Press the seams toward the large triangle in each resulting Flying Geese unit.

Flying Geese Unit
Make 48

3. Sew 3 Flying Geese units to each corner unit to make crossbars for the block.

Crossbar
Make 16

4. Sew 2 crossbars to each of the 4 center squares (Template #5), making sure that the "geese" point toward the center in each one. Press the seam toward the center square in each resulting double crossbar.

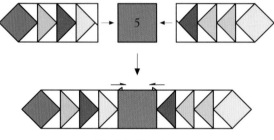

Double Crossbar
Make 4

5. Sew 2 large scrappy triangles (Template #6) to each side of the remaining crossbars.

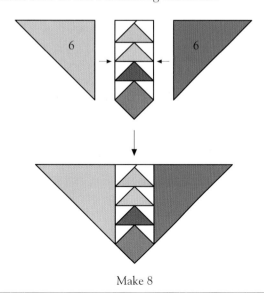

Make 8

6. Sew 2 large triangle units to opposite sides of each of the double crossbars.

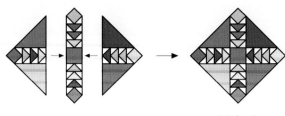

Make 4

If you prefer to rotary-cut and quick-piece the 48 Flying Geese units for this quilt, follow the cutting and sewing directions below:

1. From the scraps, cut 48 rectangles, each 2" x 3½".
2. From the white fabric, cut 96 squares, each 2" x 2".
3. Draw a diagonal line on the wrong side of each square as shown.

4. With right sides together, position and stitch a white square to one end of each scrappy rectangle as shown.

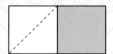

5. Trim away the corner ¼" from the stitching and discard the cutaway. Press the seam toward the rectangle.

Discard

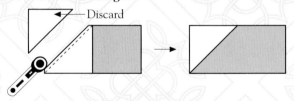

6. Repeat at the opposite end of each rectangle to complete the Flying Geese units.

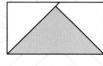

Make 48

Ninepatch Setting-Square Assembly

1. Sew 2 red squares (Template #1) to opposite sides of 18 white squares. Press the seams toward the red squares.

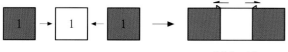

Make 18

2. Sew 2 white squares (Template #1) to opposite sides of the remaining red squares. Press the seams toward the red squares.

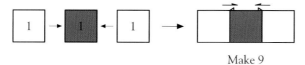

Make 9

3. Sew the units together to make a total of 9 Ninepatch blocks for the wall hanging.

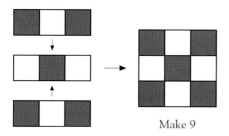

Make 9

Quilt Top Assembly and Finishing

Refer to "Assembly and Finishing Techniques," beginning on page 88.

1. Arrange the pieced blocks, the Ninepatch setting squares, and the white sashing strips in rows as shown below.

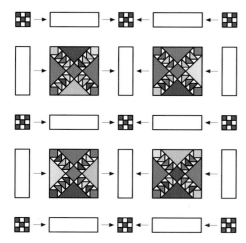

2. Sew the pieces together in rows as shown. Press all seams toward the white sashing strips.

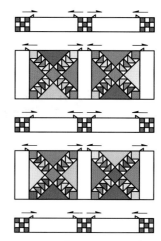

3. Sew the rows together to complete the quilt top.

4. Mark the quilting design. Mark lines on the sashing strips connecting the small squares. Mark an **X** in each medium and large square. Mark lines in each large triangle ³/₄" apart.

5. Layer the quilt top with batting and backing; baste.
6. Quilt on the marked lines. Outline-quilt the pieced triangles and the Ninepatch squares.
7. Bind the edges with white binding.
8. Add a label to your finished quilt. See page 94.

SUNFLOWER GARDEN

Quilt Dimensions: 56¹/₂" x 56¹/₂"
Shoo Fly Block Size: 6" x 6"
Sunflower Block Size: 12" x 12"

*T*he Sunflower quilt was made by Mary Copp, who was born in Woodstock, Virginia, circa 1833. She moved to Fisher's Hill, a small village near Strasburg, Virginia, at the time of her marriage. This property was the site of a Civil War battle, and the house was burned. Mrs. Copp moved to Strasburg, where she died in 1887. Her quilt was given to the Smithsonian by her granddaughter, Mrs. Irene Copp Pifer.

Mary Copp's quilt intrigued me because of the combination of patchwork patterns. The ninepatch pattern known as "Shoo Fly" is simple, while the Sunflower or Blazing Star in the borders is more complicated.

I first saw this quilt in a black-and-white photograph in the Textile Library in the Smithsonian's National Museum of American History. With the abundance of sunflower print fabrics available in the quilt shops, I couldn't wait to go home and stitch a variation in bright sunflower fabrics. It is the first quilt I stitched for this book. Was I surprised when I later saw the Smithsonian quilt "in person" in pink, brown, and blue!

The sunflowers in the original quilt have nineteen petals. Did you notice? It was much easier to draft the new pattern with sixteen petals. This also makes it easier to piece the petals into the circular background piece. If you love stitching the single Sunflower block, you may wish to create enough for the setting of the original quilt.

SUNFLOWER
quilt from the Smithsonian collection, 185.3cm x 233.2cm (73" x 91").

SUNFLOWER GARDEN
*by Mimi Dietrich, 1994, Baltimore, Maryland,
56¹/2″ x 56¹/2″. Quilted by Amish friends.*

2³/₄ yds. flower print for sunflower background, Shoo Fly block centers, outer border, and binding

1¹/₂ yds. green for Shoo Fly block triangles, sunflower background, and inner border

1¹/₂ yds. light tan for background

¹/₄ yd. light gold for small sunflower petals

³/₄ yd. bright gold for Shoo Fly block triangles and sunflower petals

¹/₈ yd. brown plaid for sunflower center

3¹/₂ yds. flower print fabric for backing

60" x 60" piece of batting

Thread

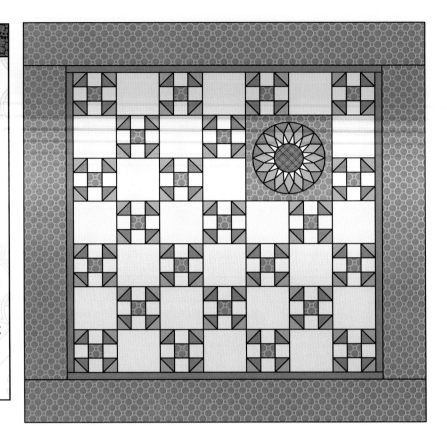

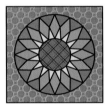

Sunflower

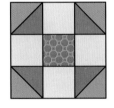

Shoo Fly

Template Cutting

Use the templates on pages 98–99.

Cut the borders first from the length of the flower print and green fabric. Use the remaining fabric to cut the pieces, using the templates.

From the flower print, cut:

2 strips, each 6¹/₂" x 44¹/₂", for the outer border

2 strips, each 6¹/₂" x 56¹/₂", for the outer border

1 square, 12¹/₂" x 12¹/₂", for the Sunflower block

23 Template #5 for the Shoo Fly blocks

From the green fabric, cut:

2 strips, each 1¹/₂" x 42¹/₂", for the inner border

2 strips, each 1¹/₂" x 44¹/₂", for the inner border

16 Template #3 for the Sunflower block

92 Template #6 for the Shoo Fly blocks

From the light tan background fabric, cut:

22 squares, each 6¹/₂" x 6¹/₂", for the setting squares

92 Template #5 for the Shoo Fly blocks

From the light gold fabric, cut:

16 Template #1 for the Sunflower block

From the bright gold fabric, cut:

16 Template #2 for the Sunflower block

92 Template #6 for the Shoo Fly blocks

From the brown plaid, cut:

1 Template #4 for the Sunflower block

Sunflower Block Assembly

1. Sew one light gold flower petal (Template #1) to each bright gold diamond petal (Template #2) as shown. Press the seams toward the bright petals.

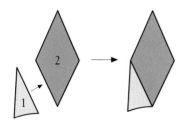

2. Sew each bright gold diamond petal to the side of a green triangle (Template #3) as shown. Press the seams toward the green triangles.

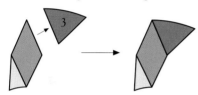

3. Sew the petal units together to make a circle, taking care to match intersecting seams. Press the seams in one direction around the circle.

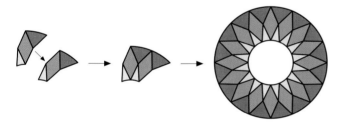

4. Cut a freezer-paper circle by tracing the *dashed lines* of Template #4 on page 99. Place the plastic-coated side of the circle on the *wrong side* of the brown plaid circle. Press. Turn and baste the seam allowance over the outer edge of the circle. Appliqué the circle to the center of the sunflower. Remove the basting and the freezer paper.

5. Fold the background square in quarters and press. Use the guide on page 99 to cut a circle in the center of the square. Staystitch a scant 1/4" from the raw edges.

Hole cut in center

Background square

6. Pin the sunflower to the background square, right sides together, with sunflower points at the pressed guidelines. Clip the background square to the stay stitching as needed. With the sunflower on top, sew together 1/4" from the raw edges. Make sure you don't sew across the petal points. Press the seam toward the background square.

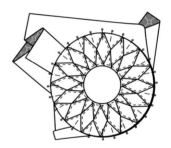

Shoo Fly Block Assembly

1. Sew each green triangle (Template #6) to a bright gold triangle (Template #6) as shown. Press the seam toward the green triangle in each resulting half-square triangle unit.

Make 92

2. For each Shoo Fly block, arrange 4 half-square triangle units with 1 sunflower square (Template #5) and 4 tan squares (Template #5) as shown, making sure the pieced squares are positioned with the gold triangles in the outer corners.

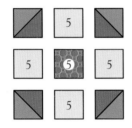

3. Sew the pieces for each block together in rows. Press the seams toward the tan squares in each row. Make 23 Shoo Fly blocks.

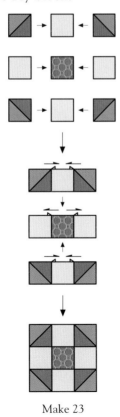

Make 23

Quilt Top Assembly and Finishing

Refer to "Assembly and Finishing Techniques," beginning on page 88.

1. Arrange the Shoo Fly blocks, plain tan setting squares, and the Sunflower block in horizontal rows as shown.

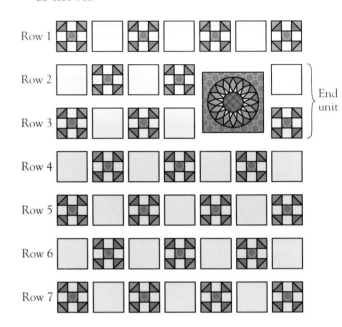

2. For Row 1 and Rows 4–7, sew the blocks and tan setting squares together in rows. Press the seams toward the tan squares.

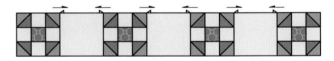

3. Repeat with the pieces for Rows 2 and 3 and with the pieces for the end unit.

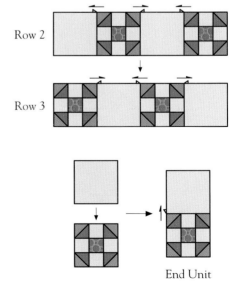

End Unit

4. Sew Rows 2 and 3 together, then add the Sunflower block to the right end, followed by the end unit. Press seams toward the Sunflower block.

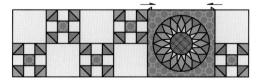

5. Sew the rows together.

6. Sew the 1½" x 42½" green inner border strips to opposite sides of the quilt top. Press the seams toward the border. Sew the remaining green border strips to the top and bottom edges of the quilt top. Press the seams toward the border.

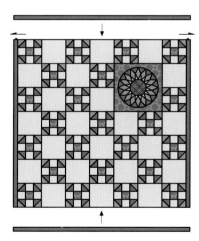

7. Sew the 6½" x 44 ½" sunflower-print outer border strips to opposite sides of the quilt top. Press the seams toward the green inner border. Sew the

remaining sunflower border strips to the top and bottom edges of the quilt. Press the seams toward the green inner border.

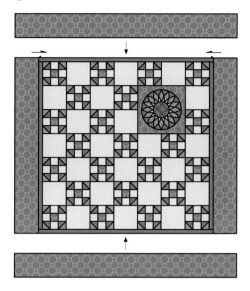

8. Mark the quilting design. Trace the Sunflower design on page 98 in the plain setting blocks. Mark a cable pattern of your choice in the outer border.
9. Layer the quilt top with batting and backing; baste.
10. Quilt on the marked lines. Quilt next to the seams on the patchwork and the green border.

11. Bind the edges with flower-print binding.
12. Add a label to your finished quilt. See page 94.

CARPENTER'S WHEEL

Quilt Dimensions: 47¹/2" x 47¹/2" ❧ Block Size: 12" x 12"

The Carpenter's Wheel quilt was pieced by Jane Winter Price of Maryland in the second quarter of the nineteenth century. The initials "JWP" are quilted into a triangle at the foot of the quilt. In addition, "Keate Price McHenry from her Mother" is written in one corner of the quilt lining. Jane Winter Price was married in 1849, when she was 30 years old. It is believed that she may have made this quilt for a previous engagement during which her fiancé died. The quilt was a gift of G. Ruth McHenry to the Smithsonian Institution.

Jane Winter Price's quilt is bordered by a beautiful multicolored chintz. The patchwork pieces reflect colors in the chintz. This design technique is used by many modern quiltmakers when selecting colors for their quilts. Choose your favorite contemporary print, then select colors from the print for your patchwork. The contemporary quilt inspired by the Smithsonian quilt is a wall hanging. The print border could be made from a decorator fabric to match the decor in your home.

The Carpenter's Wheel design is based on an eight-pointed star. Many of the pieces in this block are "set in," and perfect workmanship can be achieved with hand-piecing techniques. When you stitch two pieces together, take care to start and stop your needle precisely on the stitching lines at seam intersections as shown in the directions.

CARPENTER'S WHEEL
quilt from the Smithsonian
collection, 244.1cm x
274.5cm
(96" x 109¹/4").

CARPENTER'S WHEEL
by Mimi Dietrich, 1994, Baltimore, Maryland,
47¹/₂" x 47¹/₂". Quilted by Amish friends.

3/8 yd. red for center stars

5/8 yd. blue for wheels

3/8 yd. pink for triangles

1 1/4 yds. off-white for patchwork
background, center square,
and setting triangles

2 yds. print for border and binding

3 yds. coordinating fabric for backing

54" x 54" piece of batting

Thread

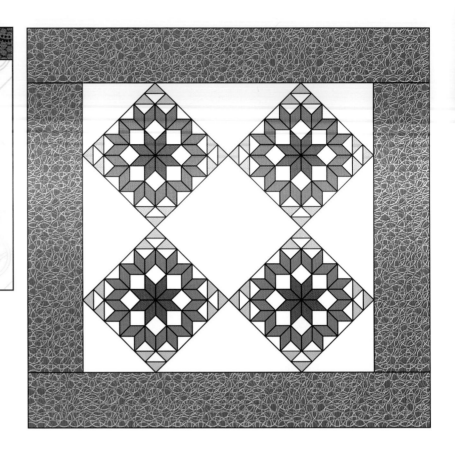

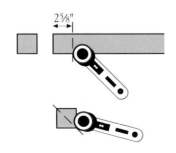

Carpenter's Wheel

Cutting

*Use the templates on page 100. Make templates
for hand piecing as directed on page 80.*

From the red fabric, cut:
32 Template #1 for the center stars in blocks

From the blue fabric, cut:
96 Template #1 for the wheels

From the pink fabric, cut:
48 Template #2. If you prefer, you can rotary-cut 2
strips, each 2 5/8" x 42", from the pink fabric. Cut a
total of 24 squares, each 2 5/8" x 2 5/8", from the strips.
Cut once diagonally for a total of 48 triangles.

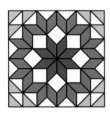

From the off-white background fabric, cut:
80 Template #2. If you prefer, you can rotary-cut
3 strips, each 2 5/8" x 42", then cut a total of 40
squares, each 2 5/8" x 2 5/8", from the strips.
Cut once diagonally as shown
below, left, for a total of 80 triangles.

32 Template #3. If you prefer, you may rotary-cut 2
strips, each 2 1/4" x 42". Cut a total of 32 squares,
each 2 1/4" x 2 1/4", from the strips.

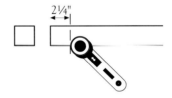

1 square, 12½" x 12½", for the quilt center

1 square, 18¼" x 18¼". Cut twice diagonally for a total of 4 side setting triangles.

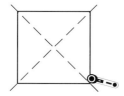

2 squares, each 9½" x 9½". Cut once diagonally for a total of 4 corner setting triangles.

From the print border fabric, cut:

2 strips, each 7" x 34½", for the side borders

2 strips, each 7" x 47½", for the top and bottom borders

Carpenter's Wheel Block Assembly

I recommend hand piecing for accuracy and ease in setting the pieces together. Mark seam lines on the wrong side of each piece. *Be very careful to begin and end all stitching at the seam-line intersections.* See "Hand Stitching Patchwork Pieces" on page 81.

Stitching lines
marked on wrong side

1. Sew 2 red diamonds (Template #1) together as shown.

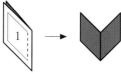

2. Sew 2 red diamond units together to make a half star as shown.

3. Sew 2 red star halves together to form the star in the center of the block. Press all of the seams in one direction around the star.

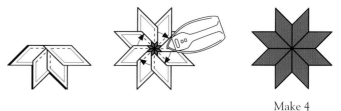

Make 4

4. Sew an off-white square (Template #3) between each of the red points as shown. Press the seams toward the squares. Repeat steps 1–4 to make a total of 4 center star units.

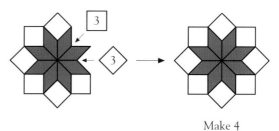

Make 4

5. Sew 3 blue diamonds together as shown. Make 8 of these blue units for each block. Press all seams in one direction.

Make 32

6. Sew the blue diamond units between the off-white squares of each center star unit as shown. Connect the blue units to form the wheel. Press the seams toward the squares.

7. Add 16 off-white triangles (Template #2) between the blue diamonds in each unit as shown. Press the seams toward the triangles.

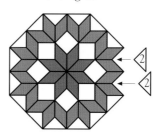

8. Sew an off-white triangle (Template #2) to each of 16 pink triangles as shown. Add 2 pink triangles to each unit.

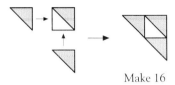

Make 16

9. Sew the pink triangle units to the corners of each block. Press the seams toward the triangle units.

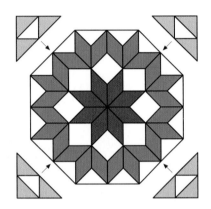

Quilt Top Assembly and Finishing

Refer to "Assembly and Finishing Techniques," beginning on page 88.

1. Arrange the pieced blocks, center setting square, and side and corner setting triangles in diagonal rows as shown. Sew the blocks and triangles together. Press the seams in opposite directions from row to row. Add the corner triangles last.

2. Sew the 7" x 34½" border strips to the sides of the quilt. Press the seams toward the border. Add the 7" x 47½" border strips to the top and bottom edges of the quilt top. Press seams toward the border.

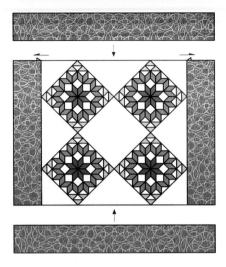

3. Mark the quilting design on the quilt top. Outline-quilt the patchwork wheels. The quilting design for the center square on page 100 was adapted from the fruit and leaves in the fabric print. You may want to use this design or trace elements from the print you have used for the borders. Coordinating quilting patterns for the setting triangles appear on the pullout pattern at the back of the book.

4. Layer the quilt top with batting and backing; baste.
5. Quilt on the marked lines.
6. Bind the edges with print binding.
7. Add a label to your finished quilt. See page 94.

SCRAP BASKETS

Quilt Dimensions: 64³/4" x 75¹/4" ~ Block Size: 7¹/2" x 7¹/2"

*T*his wonderful child's quilt from the collection at the Smithsonian's National Museum of American History was made by Keziah North Bathurst in southern Iowa or eastern Kansas circa 1885. The basket designs were pieced and appliquéd. Most of the seams were hand stitched, but some were stitched on a machine. Most of the baskets were made from the same dark, printed cotton fabric, but the baskets in the corners are of a different print, a stripe. The block setting is unusual, perhaps so that the baskets will be right side up when the quilt hangs over the edges of a bed.

This quilt has a lovely story. Keziah Bathurst was the second wife of Roland Curtis Bathurst. She made quilts for her three stepchildren, using fabrics from their own mother's dresses. She also made quilts for her children, using fabrics from her dresses. This Basket quilt was made for her stepson, Samuel Harvey Bathurst, using dresses owned by his mother, Emily Susan Bathurst. Samuel's daughter, Dr. Effie G. Bathurst, gave this quilt to the Smithsonian.

The basket design was a popular pattern for nineteenth-century quilts. Baskets often symbolize prosperity. For contemporary quilters, baskets are often the best place for storing fabric and their latest projects.

The new Scrap Baskets quilt was made from a collection of homespun plaids in rich, dark country colors. The setting is a more traditional on-point design. A contemporary quilt would look equally charming in 1930s fabrics or scraps from your favorite projects. It would be perfect for pastel fabrics left over from sewing projects for your daughter or granddaughter. Why not search through your own collection of scraps and choose fabrics for each basket that recall special memories?

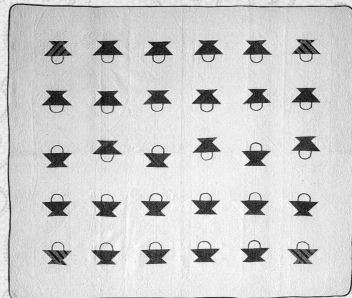

BASKET
quilt from the Smithsonian collection, 195.0cm x 166.7cm (77¹/4" x 65¹/2").

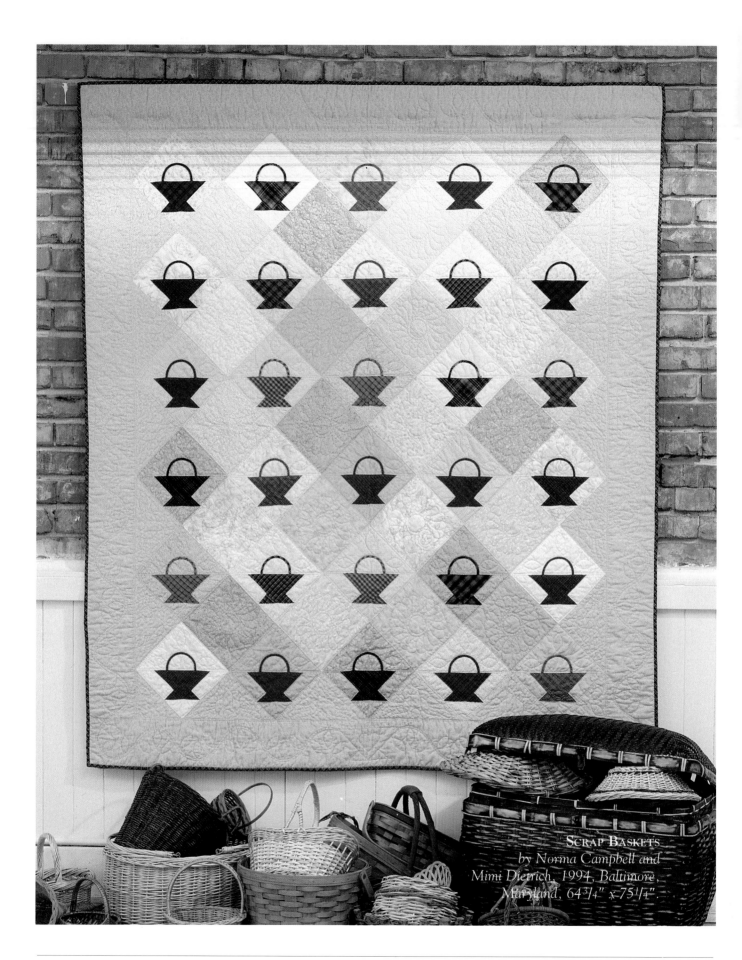

SCRAP BASKETS
by Norma Campbell and
Mimi Dietrich, 1994, Baltimore,
Maryland, 64³/₄" x 75¹/₄".

³/8 yd. each of 15 assorted background fabrics for patchwork blocks and setting squares*

3¼ yds. tan for setting triangles and border

¼ yd. each of 15 assorted plaids

4½ yds. coordinating fabric for backing

¾ yd. plaid for binding

70" x 80" piece of batting

Thread

*If you wish, you may make this quilt so that the block backgrounds all match the setting triangles and borders. In that case, buy an additional 3 yards of the tan fabric you have chosen for the setting triangles and border.

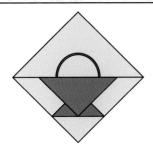

Scrap Basket

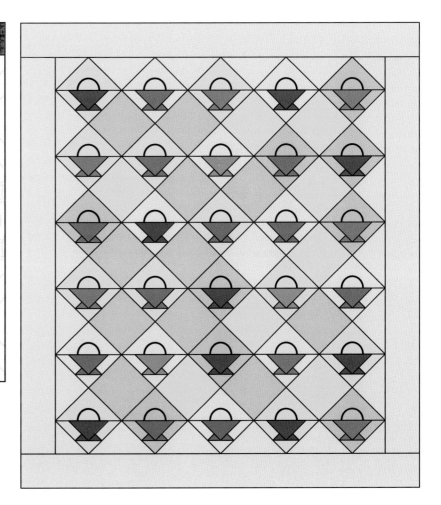

Cutting

Use the templates on pages 101–102.

From the assorted background fabrics, cut:
20 squares, each 8" x 8", for the setting squares

From the tan fabric for setting triangles and border, cut:
4 border strips, each 6" x 70", for the border; you will cut them to fit later.

5 squares, each 11⁷/8" x 11⁷/8". Cut the squares twice diagonally for a total of 20 triangles. You need only 18 of these side setting triangles.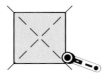

2 squares, each 6¼" x 6¼". Cut the squares once diagonally for a total of 4 corner setting triangles.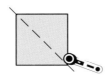

For *each* block, cut the following pieces. You will need to cut pieces for a total of 30 blocks.

From the plaid fabric, cut:
1 Template #1

2 Template #2

1 bias strip, ³/4" x 7"

From the assorted background fabrics, cut:
1 Template #3

1 Template #4

1 Template #4 reversed

1 Template #5

Basket Block Assembly

1. Arrange the basket and background pieces for each block as shown.

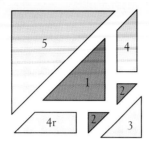

2. Sew the small plaid triangles (Template #2) to the background pieces (Templates #4 and #4 reversed). Press the seams toward the plaid triangles.

Make 1 for each block.

Make 1 for each block.

3. Sew the resulting units to the large plaid triangle (Template #1). Press the seam toward the plaid triangle.

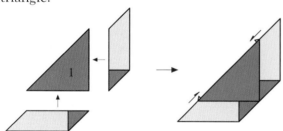

4. Sew the small background triangle (Template #3) to the bottom of the "basket." Press the seam toward the triangle.

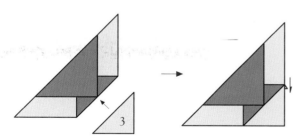

5. Trace the handle placement line onto the large background triangle (Template #5).

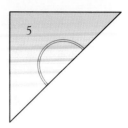

6. To prepare the basket handle, fold the plaid bias strip in half lengthwise, wrong sides together. Press with a steam iron or baste close to the raw edges.

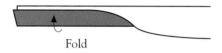

7. Position the raw edges of the handle just inside the upper placement line.

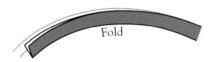

8. Using small running stitches, sew the strip to the background, positioning the stitches slightly away from the center of the strip, toward the raw edges.

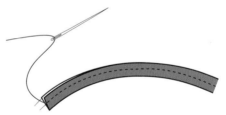

9. Roll the folded edge over the seam allowance. Appliqué the fold to the background fabric to create a smooth handle.

10. Sew the large triangle to the top of the basket. Press the seam toward the basket.

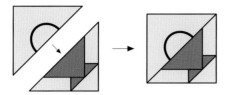

11. Repeat steps 1–10 to make a total of 30 Basket blocks.

Quilt Top Assembly and Finishing

Refer to "Assembly and Finishing Techniques," beginning on page 88.

1. Arrange the Basket blocks, the setting squares, and the tan side and corner setting triangles in diagonal rows as shown. Choose the basket setting you prefer: the baskets to the side as in the Smithsonian setting or all baskets on point and straight as in the new quilt. Sew the blocks and triangles together in diagonal rows. Press all seams toward the background setting blocks. Sew the rows together, adding the corner triangles last.

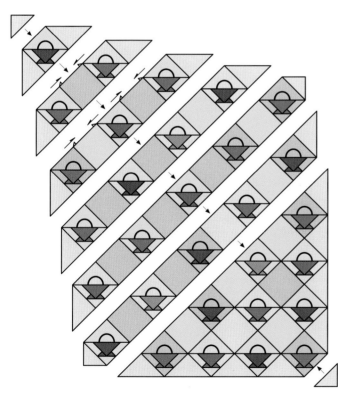

2. Measure the quilt top for borders with straight-cut corners. (See page 89–90.) Cut 2 border strips to fit the length of the quilt and sew one to each long side. Press seams toward the border. Measure for, trim, and sew border strips to the top and bottom edges.

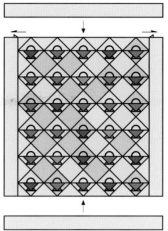

3. Mark the quilting designs on the quilt top, using the patterns on pages 101 and 103–106 and referring to the illustration below for placement. Outline-quilt the baskets. Mark feathered wreaths in the plain setting blocks. Mark the bird design from the original quilt in the setting triangles. Mark vines with leaves and baskets in the border. Use the leaf pattern from the corner setting triangles in the upper half of each Basket block as shown.

4. Layer the quilt top with batting and backing; baste.
5. Quilt on the marked lines.
6. Bind the edges with plaid binding.
7. Add a label to your finished quilt. See page 94.

CHIPS AND WHETSTONES

Quilt Dimensions: 42¹/₂" x 42¹/₂" ✦ Block Size: 18" x 18"

*T*his masterpiece Smithsonian quilt was made in the third quarter of the nineteenth century. The twenty circular pieced star patterns were combined with appliquéd flowers where the block corners join. The Chips and Whetstones pattern takes us back to a time when a woodsman chopped trees by hand. He carried a whetstone to sharpen his ax. The large, dark points of the star represent the whetstones, and the small pieces surrounding the points represent wood chips cut from trees.

When all of the large points in this design are cut from dark fabrics, this pattern is also known as Mariner's Compass. This name may have been suggested to East Coast quiltmakers by the compass rose found on early sea charts. The compass rose was divided into as few as four points indicating the compass directions, with as many as thirty-two points on more intricate designs.

I love the combination of pieced and appliquéd designs in this quilt. Hearts appliquéd to each corner of each block create the flowers when the blocks are joined.

The modern quilt was made to imitate the scrappy "feel" of the old quilt. The red fabric used in the hearts gives continuity to the overall design. Each star was made in different color combinations from the 1994 Smithsonian Quilt Fabric Collection®, produced by RJR Fashion Fabrics. This fabric collection was inspired by quilts made during the same period as the special quilt shown at right.

CHIPS AND WHETSTONES *quilt from the Smithsonian collection, 198.7cm x 242.2cm (78" x 95¹/₈").*

CHIPS AND WHETSTONES
by Pat Brousil, 1994, Columbia,
Maryland, 42$\frac{1}{2}$" x 42$\frac{1}{2}$".
Quilted by Amish Friends.

MATERIALS: 44"-WIDE FABRIC

2 yds. for background

1/2 yd. light red print for border

3/4 yd. red for hearts and binding

4 sets of 1/8-yd. to 1/4-yd.
pieces for blocks. Each block
requires 5 coordinating fabrics:
1 floral print,
1 dark print, 1 light print,
and 2 medium prints.

1 3/8 yds. coordinating fabric for backing

44" x 44" piece of batting

Thread

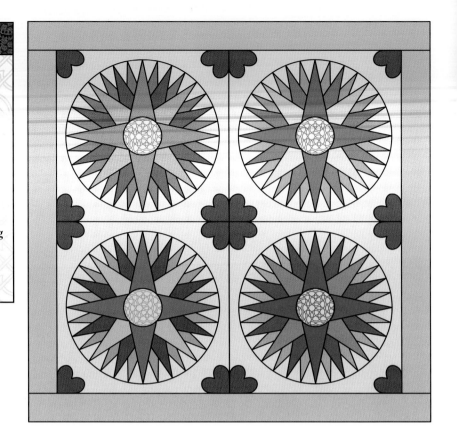

Chips and Whetstones

Cutting

Use the templates on pages 107–108.
Cut the pieces from each fabric in the order listed.

From the background fabric, cut:
4 squares, each 18 1/2" x 18 1/2",
for the background blocks

128 Template #1

From the light red print, cut:
2 strips, each 3 1/2" x 36 1/2", for the side borders

2 strips, each 3 1/2" x 42 1/2",
for the top and bottom borders

From the red fabric, cut:
16 hearts (Template #7)

From each of 4 medium prints #1, cut:
16 Template #2 for a total of 64

From each of 4 medium prints #2, cut:
8 Template #3 for a total of 32

From each of the 4 light prints, cut:
4 Template #4 for a total of 16

From each of the 4 dark prints, cut:
4 Template #5 for a total of 16

From each of the 4 floral prints, cut:
1 Template #6

Chips and Whetstones
Block Assembly

The Chips and Whetstones patchwork is constructed from the outside edge, moving toward the center and adding the center circle last. You may piece this pattern by hand or machine. Accurate stitching is essential so that each completed circle lies flat.

1. Sew 2 background pieces (Template #1) to 1 of the medium print #1 pieces (Template #2) as shown. Press the seam toward the background. Make 16 of these outer-edge units for each block.

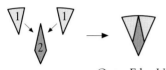

Outer-Edge Unit
Make 16 for each block.

2. Sew 2 outer-edge units to each medium print #2 piece (Template #3) as shown. Press the seam toward the edge unit. Make 8 of these units for each block.

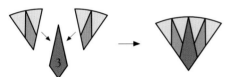

Make 8 for each block.

3. Sew 2 of the units from step 2 to each light-print piece (Template #4). Press the seams toward the pieced unit. Make 4 of these quarter units for each block.

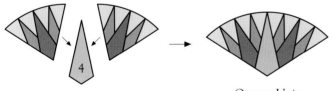

Quarter Unit
Make 4 for each block.

4. Sew 2 quarter units to each dark-print piece (Template #5). Press the seam away from the dark-print piece in each unit. Make 2 of these half units for each block.

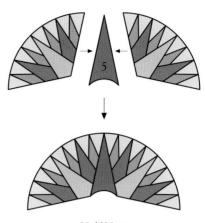

Half Unit
Make 2 for each block.

5. Sew the half units to the remaining dark-print pieces to finish the circle for each block.

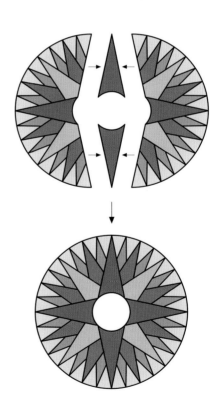

6. Make a freezer-paper circle by tracing the dashed lines of Template #6 on page 108. Cut out. Place the coated side of the freezer paper on the wrong side of the floral-print fabric for the center. Iron in place with a warm, dry iron. Turn under and baste the seam allowance over the outer edge of the freezer-paper circle.

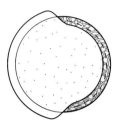

7. Appliqué the circle to the center of the design. Remove the basting and the freezer paper.

8. Fold the 18½" background squares in quarters and press. Use the Center Cutting guide on the pullout pattern at the back of the book to mark and cut a circle out of the center of each square.

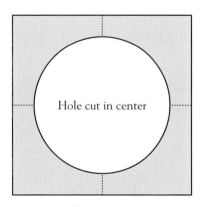

Background square

9. With right sides together, pin each circle to a background square, matching the dark-print points of the pieced circle to the pressed marks in the background square.

With the circle on top, stitch the background and circle together, using a ¼"-wide seam allowance. Be careful not to stitch across the points. Press the seam toward the background square.

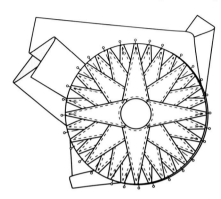

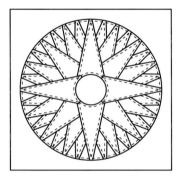

10. Clip each heart *almost* to the stitching line at the dot on each side of the point.

11. Turn and appliqué the outer curved edges of the hearts in place at each corner of each block. Cut away the background behind the hearts.

Wrong side of heart

Quilt Top Assembly and Finishing

Refer to "Assembly and Finishing Techniques," beginning on page 88.

1. Arrange the 4 blocks as shown. Sew together in horizontal rows; press seams in opposite directions. Join the rows, making sure that the hearts match at the seam intersections.

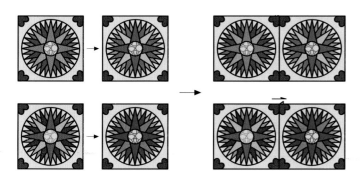

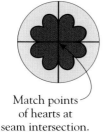

Match points of hearts at seam intersection.

2. Sew the 3¹/₂" x 36¹/₂" border strips to the sides of the quilt. Press the seams toward the border. Sew the remaining border strips to the top and bottom edges of the quilt top. Press the seams toward the border.

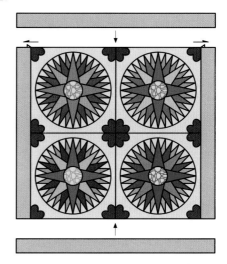

3. Mark the quilting design on the quilt top. Mark circles ¹/₂" apart around the pieced designs. Mark ¹/₄" inside the red hearts. Mark hearts on the light red border.
4. Layer the quilt top with batting and backing; baste.
5. Quilt on the marked lines. Quilt ¹/₈" inside points. Quilt as desired in the floral-print center circle.

6. Bind the edges with red binding.
7. Add a label to your finished quilt. See page 94.

SPRING TULIPS

Quilt Dimensions: 26½" x 26½"   Block Size: 8" x 8"

Many nineteenth-century quilts reflect the quilters' love of flowers. Tulips are a favorite motif often found stitched into the designs of various floral quilts. Just imagine the joy of appliquéing spring flowers as you await the end of a long, cold winter!

Very little is known about this vibrant Tulip quilt from the collection at the Smithsonian. It is made of cotton and dated in the third quarter of the nineteenth century. It was a gift of Mrs. Roy E. Thomas and Col. Herbert A. Meek.

The contemporary wall hanging was adapted from the original Smithsonian quilt with a few design changes. First, the patterns given here are for blocks that finish to 8" square, half of the original block size. If you wish to stitch them in the original size, use modern technology and enlarge the pattern 200% on a photocopier.

Instead of the nineteenth-century colors, the new quilt has purple tulips, inspired by the contemporary fabric used for the outer border. In addition, the maker used the border fabric in the appliqués for added sparkle in the tulips. The setting design was also simplified for uncomplicated borders. The only templates you will need for this easy quilt are for the tulips and leaves. Have fun creating a small wall hanging so you can enjoy spring tulips all year long.

TULIP
quilt from the Smithsonian collection, 201cm x 201cm (79" x 79").

SPRING TULIPS
by Eleanor Eckman, 1994,
Baltimore, Maryland, 26¹/₂″ x 26¹/₂″.
Quilted by Amish friends.

MATERIALS: 44"-WIDE FABRIC

$3/8$ yd. off-white for background

$3/8$ yd. dark purple for tulips
and inner border

$1/4$ yd. light purple solid for
tulips and center square

$5/8$ yd. green for stems,
leaves, and binding

1 yd. print for appliqué details,
center triangles, and outer border

1 yd. coordinating fabric for backing

30" x 30" piece of batting

Thread

Tulip

Cutting

*Make appliqué templates for the tulips and leaves
by tracing the required shapes from the pattern on
page 109. Choose your favorite appliqué method from
those given in "Appliqué," beginning on page 83.*

From the off-white background fabric, cut:
4 squares, each $8^1/2$" x $8^1/2$", for the
block backgrounds

4 strips, each $1^1/2$" x $8^1/2$", for the
sashing between blocks

From the dark purple, cut:
2 strips, each 1" x $17^1/2$", for the inner side borders

2 strips, each 1" x $18^1/2$", for the
inner top and bottom borders

4 each of pieces 14, 17, and 20

From the light purple solid, cut:
4 each of pieces 10 and 12

4 each of pieces 15, 18, and 21

1 square, $1^1/2$" x $1^1/2$", for the quilt center

From the green fabric, cut:
8 bias strips, each $1/2$" x 3", for the
short tulip stems (pieces 1 and 2)

4 bias strips, each $5/8$" x 6", for the
long tulip stems (piece 3)

8 large leaves (pieces 4 and 5)

16 small leaves (pieces 6–9)

4 each of pieces 11 and 13

**From the print for
appliqués and border, cut:**
2 strips, each $4^1/2$" x $18^1/2$",
for the outer side borders

2 strips, each $4^1/2$" x $26^1/2$", for
the outer top and bottom borders

4 each of pieces 16, 19, 22, and 23

Tulip Block Appliqué

1. Fold each of the four background squares in quarters to find the center point. Crease. Place each square over the appliqué pattern on page 109 and trace the design, using a sharp pencil. See "Marking the Design on the Background Blocks" on page 84.

2. Fold each of the long and short green stem strips in half lengthwise, wrong sides together. Press with a steam iron or baste close to the raw edges.

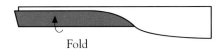

Fold

3. Position the raw edges of stems 1 and 2 just inside the longer of the two curved placement lines.

Fold

4. Using small running stitches, sew the strips to the background through the center of each strip.

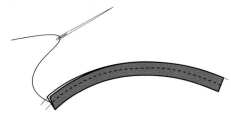

5. Roll the folded edge over the seam allowance. Appliqué the fold to the background fabric to create a smooth stem.

6. Appliqué a long stem 3 to each block, covering the raw edges of stems 1 and 2.

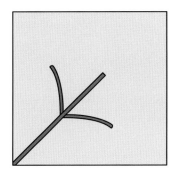

7. Appliqué the leaves, buds, and tulips to the blocks in numerical order. In order to properly position the tulip centers, make a pattern "window." Trace the tulip design on a piece of paper. Cut out the center design, forming the window. Place this over the tulip and drop the center piece in place.

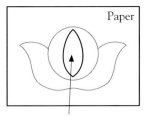

Paper

Cut out for placement window.

8. When you appliqué the triangle at the corner of the block, stitch the long edge only. Let the other sides lie flat against the background fabric and baste them in place.

Appliqué this edge.

Quilt Top Assembly and Finishing

Refer to "Assembly and Finishing Techniques," beginning on page 88.

1. Arrange the appliquéd blocks, background sashing strips, and center square in rows as shown, making sure the tulips "grow" out from the center.

2. Sew the pieces together in rows; press the seams toward the sashing strips.

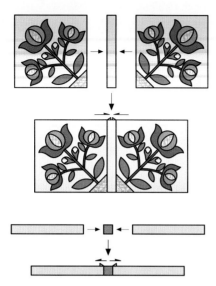

3. Sew the rows together.

4. Sew the 1" x 17½" purple border strips to the sides of the quilt and press the seams toward the border. Sew the remaining purple border strips to the top and bottom edges of the quilt top. Press seams toward the border.

5. Add the 4½" x 18½" print border strips to the sides of the quilt and press the seams toward the purple border. Sew the remaining print border strips to the top and bottom edges of the quilt top and press the seams toward the purple border.

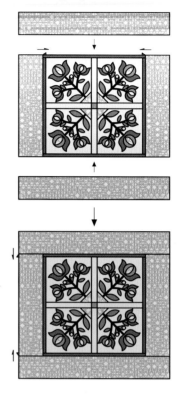

6. Mark the quilting design on the quilt top. Mark a grid of diagonal lines spaced ³/4" apart, marking the center diagonal lines first.

7. Layer the quilt top with batting and backing; baste.
8. Quilt on the marked lines. Outline-quilt around the appliqués.
9. Bind the edges with green binding.
10. Add a label to your finished quilt. See page 94.

ALL-AMERICAN EAGLE

Quilt Dimensions: 42½" x 42½"
Center Size: 30" x 30"   Block Size: 6" x 6"

The original Eagle quilt was pieced and appliquéd in the first quarter of the nineteenth century. The quilt belonged to the Dove-Cator family in Baltimore and Harford Counties in Maryland. It was given to the Smithsonian by Mrs. Carrie T. Brown.

The center panel of the Smithsonian quilt is an appliquéd eagle holding arrows and an olive branch. It is surrounded by a row of pieced Star blocks and appliquéd Crossed Leaves blocks. The rest of the large quilt consists of alternating pieced Star blocks and plain white blocks.

The eagle and stars have long been symbols of national pride and patriotism. The olive branches symbolize peace, and the arrows strength. The star pattern appeared in quilts as early as the late 1700s and has been known by such names as Variable Star and Ohio Star.

The new quilt is a wall hanging adapted from the center of the Eagle quilt and the surrounding row of pieced and appliquéd blocks. The fabrics in the original quilt were block-printed and roller-printed florals and geometrics in red, blue, and brown. The old quilt has a soft chintz quality. The new quilt was made in bold country colors, complementing the paisley eagle fabric and the tan background fabric.

Stitch this spirited wall hanging for a grand Fourth of July celebration, or make a larger quilt for a special patriotic commemoration!

EAGLE
quilt from the Smithsonian collection, 183.9cm x 224.8cm (72½" x 88½").

ALL-AMERICAN EAGLE
by Penny Clifton, Mimi Dietrich, Sherry Fulkoski, Diana Harper,
Marian Nozinski, Barbara Roberts, Libbie Rollman, Christine Russell, Dawn Schaefer,
Fran Timmins, and Carol Watson, 1994, Baltimore, Maryland, 42¹/₂" x 42¹/₂".
Quilted by Amish friends.

2¼ yds. for background
¾ yd. print for eagle
1¼ yds. green for leaves
⅜ yd. gold for stars and arrows
¼ yd. blue for star centers
1 yd. red for stars and binding
1¼ yds. coordinating fabric for backing
45" x 45" piece of batting
Thread

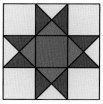

Star   Crossed Leaves

Cutting

*Use the templates on page 96 and on
the pullout patterns at the back of the book.
Cut the pieces from each fabric in the order listed.*

From the background fabric, cut:
1 square, 30½" x 30½", for the eagle background

12 squares, each 6½" x 6½",
for the Crossed Leaves blocks

48 Template #1, for the Star blocks. If you prefer,
rotary-cut 3 strips, each 2½" x 42". Cut a total of 48
squares, each 2½" x 2½", from the strips.

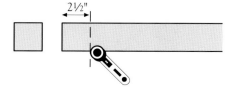

48 Template #2 for the Star blocks.
If you prefer, rotary-cut 1 strip, 3¼" x 42".
Cut a total of 12 squares, each 3¼" x 3¼".
If your fabric is not at least 42" wide, you will
need to cut 1 additional square from scraps.
Cut the squares twice diagonally for 48 triangles.

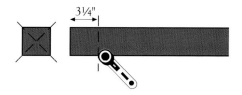

From the print fabric for the eagle, cut:
1 square, 24" x 24"

From the green fabric, cut:

11 small leaves, 2 stems, 2 large branches, and 4 corner leaves, using freezer-paper templates traced from the full-size pattern on the pullout pattern. See "Freezer-Paper Appliqué" on pages 87–88.

24 leaves, using freezer-paper templates traced from Template #3 on page 96. Mark the center on each freezer-paper leaf. Place the templates on the bias grain of the fabric, and the curves will turn under easily. Be sure to press the freezer paper to the right side of the fabric for "Appliqué with Freezer Paper on Top," page 88. Cut out 1/4" away from the paper edges.

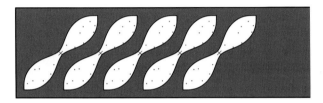

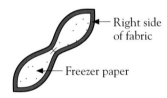

Right side of fabric

Freezer paper

From the gold fabric, cut:

48 Template #2, for the Star blocks. If you prefer, rotary-cut 1 strip, 3¹/4" x 42". Cut a total of 12 squares, each 3¹/4" x 3¹/4". If your fabric is not at least 42" wide, you will need to cut 1 additional square from scraps. Cut the squares twice diagonally as shown on page 47, for 48 triangles.

5 strips, each ¹/2" x 8", for the arrows

5 triangle arrow points, using freezer-paper templates traced from the pattern

From the blue fabric, cut:

12 Template #1 for the Star blocks. If you prefer, rotary-cut 1 strip, 2¹/2" x 42". Cut a total of 12 squares, each 2¹/2" x 2¹/2", from the strip.

From the red fabric, cut:

96 Template #2 for the Star blocks. If you prefer, rotary-cut 2 strips, each 3¹/4" x 42". If your fabric is not at least 42" wide, you will need to cut 2 additional squares from scraps. Cut a total of 24 squares, each 3¹/4" x 3¹/4", from the strips. Cut twice diagonally as shown above for a total of 96 triangles.

Eagle Block Assembly

1. Trace the eagle pattern (on 2 pullout pattern pages at the back of the book) onto the *uncoated* side of freezer paper. Trace the dashed lines that mark the center of the eagle. Cut out the freezer-paper eagle. Cut out the chest markings.

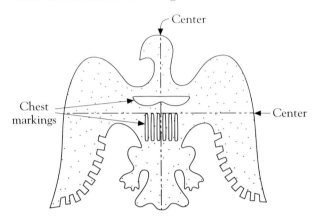

Center

Chest markings

Center

2. Fold the 30¹/2" x 30¹/2" background fabric square in quarters and press to mark the center.

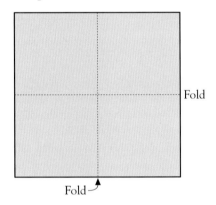

Fold

Fold

3. Fold the 24" x 24" eagle-print fabric in quarters and press to mark the center positioning lines. With the right side of the print square face up, position the freezer-paper eagle on top, aligning the center marks with the creases. Iron in place with a warm, dry iron.

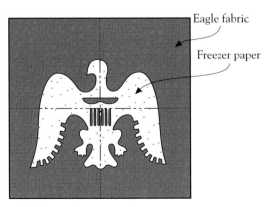

Eagle fabric

Freezer paper

4. Place the eagle-print fabric over the background fabric, matching the center folds. Baste the print to the background square around the outside edges. Baste 3/8" in from the paper edges through all layers.

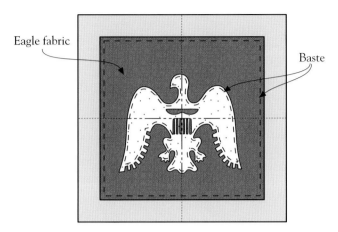

Eagle fabric

Baste

5. *Being careful to cut only the print fabric,* cut 1/4" away from the outer edge of the freezer-paper eagle, cutting only 2" at a time. Turn under the edge and sew in place as shown for "Appliqué with Freezer Paper on Top" on page 88.

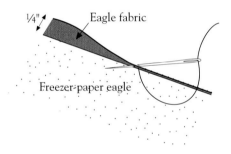

1/4"

Eagle fabric

Freezer-paper eagle

6. To appliqué the chest details, cut 1/8" to 1/4" away from the freezer paper, cutting the top layer of fabric only. Clip curves as needed for a smoothly turned edge. Turn cut edges under, even with the freezer-paper edge, and stitch in place. This is reverse appliqué.

7. Remove the basting stitches and the excess print fabric. Peel the freezer paper away to reveal the appliquéd eagle.
8. Position the background square over the pullout pattern. Trace the leaves and arrows onto the background fabric. If you cannot see through the fabric, place the pattern and fabric over a light box or against a large, sunny window.
9. Iron the large freezer-paper leaves onto the green fabric. Appliqué the large leaves in place on the background fabric.
10. Appliqué the stems and small leaves.
11. Fold the raw edges in to meet in the center of each of the 1/2" x 8" gold strips. Baste along the folded edges. Trim each strip to the correct length—1/4" longer than the pattern marking at each end.

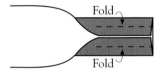

Fold

Fold

12. Appliqué the strips to the background fabric, turning under the tops to finish the edges. Appliqué the arrow points over the bottom raw ends of the shafts.

Crossed Leaves Block Assembly

1. Fold each 6 1/2" background square diagonally into quarters as shown. Finger-press to crease.

2. Pin a leaf with freezer-paper pattern still attached to the background fabric, matching the center mark to the folded center and the leaf points to the folded line.

3. Turn the seam allowance under the edge of the freezer paper and appliqué to the background fabric. Pull away the freezer paper.
4. Position another leaf across the first, matching the center and points. Appliqué to the background fabric. Remove the freezer paper. Make a total of 12 Crossed Leaves blocks in this manner.

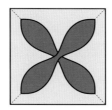

Make 12

Star Block Assembly

1. Sew a red triangle (Template #2) to a gold triangle.

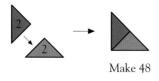

Make 48

2. Sew a red triangle to each of the background triangles.

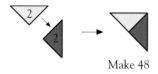

Make 48

3. Sew the triangle units together to make squares.

Make 48

4. For each of 12 blocks, arrange the pieced, blue, and background squares (Template #1) in rows as shown to form a star.

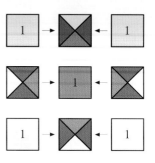

5. Sew the squares together in rows and press the seams toward the plain squares in each row. Sew the rows together.

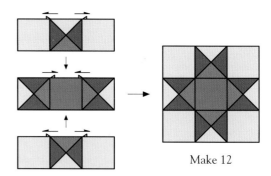

Make 12

Quilt Top Assembly and Finishing

Refer to "Assembly and Finishing Techniques," beginning on page 88.

1. Sew the Star and Crossed Leaves blocks together in vertical rows for the sides of the Eagle block and in horizontal rows for the top and bottom edges of the Eagle block. Press the seams toward the Crossed Leaves blocks.

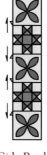

Side Border
Make 2

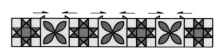

Top and Bottom Borders
Make 2

2. Sew the side rows to the Eagle block, then add the top and bottom rows.

3. Mark the quilting design on the quilt top, referring to the illustration below. In the center Eagle block, draw diagonal lines on the background fabric. Draw radiating lines from the center to the border-block seams and to the centers of each border block.
4. Layer the quilt top with batting and backing; baste.
5. Quilt on the marked lines. Outline-quilt around the appliquéd pieces. Quilt next to the seams on the patchwork stars.
6. Bind the edges with red binding.
7. Add a label to your finished quilt. See page 94.

CHESAPEAKE ROSE

Quilt Dimensions: 96¹/₂" x 96¹/₂" ✿ Block Size: 24" x 24"

This Rose of Sharon quilt in the Smithsonian collection was made in the mid-nineteenth century. The red, green, pink, and yellow cottons were skillfully appliquéd on a white cotton background, but the stuffed quilting is the most incredible feature. It is breathtaking!

The quilt was made without an overall batting or filling, but each of the quilt design areas was stuffed with cotton. The four large white squares were quilted and stuffed with a different beautiful design in each: an eagle with shield and flag, an eagle with arrows and olive branch, a grapevine, and a basket of fruit. The background was closely quilted in rows of stitches spaced only ¹/₈" apart.

The name Rose of Sharon was taken from a famous love song, the biblical verse in the Song of Solomon: "I am the rose of Sharon, and the lily of the valleys. As the lily among thorns, so is my love among the daughters." Designs with roses, leaves, and buds emanating from a large central rose are also known by names such as Whig Rose, Harrison Rose, and Democrat Rose.

Nineteenth-century appliqué artists used traditional methods to appliqué their designs. The Chesapeake Rose quilt on page 53 was made using modern freezer-paper appliqué techniques.

Chesapeake Rose was made by friends of mine who live in Maryland towns and cities along the Chesapeake Bay. Each person stitched an element in the quilt and in the border, rather than each one completing individual blocks. This gives the quilt a very consistent look. The blocks were passed around, sent back and forth, and appliquéd in about two months!

ROSE OF SHARON
quilt from the Smithsonian collection, 241.2cm x 237.2cm (95¹/₈" x 93¹/₂").

CHESAPEAKE ROSE
by Anita Askins, Norma Campbell, Toni Carr,
Jan Carlson, Mimi Dietrich, Kathy Siuta,
and Kay Twit, 1994, Baltimore, Maryland,
96$^{1}/_{2}$" x 96$^{1}/_{2}$". Quilted by Didi Salvatierra.

3½ yds. green for leaves and stems

4½ yds. red for flowers and swags

½ yd. pink for flower petals

1 yd. gold for flower centers

11¼ yds. for background and binding*

9 yds. coordinating fabric for backing

100" x 100" piece of batting

Thread

*Cut the fabric into the lengths listed under the cutting directions for the background fabric *before prewashing*. Short pieces are easier to handle than one long one.

Chesapeake Rose

Pattern Making

1. A quarter-block pattern for the Chesapeake Rose block and the border pattern appear on the pullout pattern at the back of the book. To make a full block pattern, trace the block design onto four 12" squares of graph paper. Tape the 4 pieces of paper together to form one large 24"-square pattern.

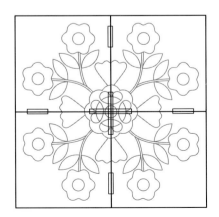

2. To make the full border pattern, cut a piece of freezer paper 96" long. Fold the freezer paper in half to find the center. Referring to the illustration below, trace the design elements on the pullout pattern onto the freezer-paper strip to make a pattern for half of the border. Fold the paper in half, tape the pattern to a large window, then trace it in reverse. Open the freezer paper to form a 96"-long border pattern.

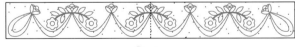

Center

Background and Border Cutting

1. Cut the 11¼-yard piece of background fabric into the following lengths; *then prewash.*

   1 piece, 1¼ yards long for the binding. Label it "Binding for Rose Quilt" and set aside. You won't need it for awhile!

   1 piece, 1 yard long
   3 pieces, each 3 yards long

2. From the 1-yard piece, cut 1 background square, 26½" x 26½". (The finished square for the quilt will be cut down to 24½" square, but it helps to work with a larger square, then trim it before assembling the quilt.) To cut an accurate square, fold the fabric into quarters and cut a 13¼" square with a rotary cutter and a large square ruler.

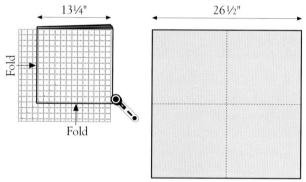

3. Using only 1 of the 3-yard pieces, cut 3 border strips, each 12½" wide and the length of the fabric. (The borders are longer than needed. You will trim them to fit later.)

4. Cut 1 additional 12½"-wide border strip from 1 of the remaining 3-yard pieces of background fabric.

5. From the remaining background fabric, cut 8 squares, each 26½" x 26½", for the block backgrounds.

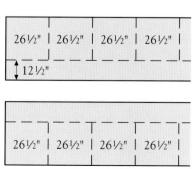

Appliqué Cutting

Use the appliqué patterns on pages 111–12 and the pattern pullout at the back of the book. Make appliqué templates for the blocks and border by tracing the template pieces onto template plastic. Use templates to cut the required number of pieces from the appropriate fabrics. If you prefer freezer-paper appliqué, trace the template shapes onto the uncoated side of freezer paper and cut out on the lines. See pages 87–88. You will need one freezer-paper shape for each appliqué piece required. Iron the freezer-paper patterns to the *wrong* side of the appropriate fabric and cut ¼" away from the outer edges of the freezer-paper shape.

Note: The pattern for the flower centers in the blocks and borders has two numbers (4/8) to designate order of appliqué, depending on which flower you are stitching.

For the blocks, cut the following pieces.
From the green fabric, cut:
36 large leaves (Template #1)

144 small leaves (Template #2)

36 bias strips, each 1" x 5", for the short stems

36 bias strips, each 1" x 6½", for the longer stems

From the red fabric, cut:
72 roses (Template #3)

9 large flowers (Template #5)

From the pink fabric, cut:
72 flower petals (Template #6)

From the gold fabric, cut:
81 flower centers (Templates #4/8)

36 flower wedges (Template #7)

For the borders, cut the following pieces.
From the green fabric, cut:
72 leaves (Template #2)

48 flower leaves (Template #12)

12 bias strips, each 1" x 14", for the stems

From the red fabric, cut:
24 border swags (Trace template from border pattern on pullout at back of book.)

4 border corner swags (Trace template from border pattern on pullout.)

24 roses (Template #3)

24 rosebuds (Template #9)

From the pink fabric, cut:
24 flower petals (Template #10)

24 flower petals (Template #10 reversed)

From the gold fabric, cut:
24 flower centers (Template #4)

24 center wedges (Template #11)

Block and Border Appliqué

1. Fold each of the 9 background squares into quarters to find the center point. Match this point to the center of the appliqué pattern on the pullout pattern and trace the design onto each of the background squares.

2. To mark the borders, center the border strips over the border pattern (step 2, page 54) and trace the swags and flowers onto each of the 4 pieces of fabric. *Do not trace the corner designs yet.*

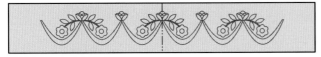

Center

3. Appliqué the stems on the blocks and borders first, using the "bias bar" technique. Fold the 1"-wide stems in half lengthwise, wrong sides together, and machine stitch ¼" from the raw edges, making a tube. Slip a ¼"-wide bias bar into the tube and position it with the seam centered on one side. Trim the seam allowance so that it does not extend past the folded edge of the strip. Press the strip flat with a steam iron, pressing the seam allowance to one side.

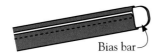

Bias bar

4. Remove the bias bar. Position the tube on the background fabric with the seam allowance next to the background fabric. Pin or baste the stem in place, then stitch both folded edges in place.

5. Appliqué the remaining pieces to the blocks in numerical order, using either traditional or freezer-paper appliqué. Refer to the patterns on the pullout. See "Appliqué," beginning on page 83. Refer to "Appliqué Tips" in the box below.

6. Referring to the pullout pattern for the border, appliqué stems and pieces 1–4 to each border strip in numerical order. Do not appliqué the corners yet. Appliqué pieces 9–12 to each border strip.

Appliqué Tips

- **To properly position the gold centers on the roses, make a window pattern. Trace the rose design onto a piece of paper. Cut out the center circle, forming a window. Place this over the rose and drop the center in place.**

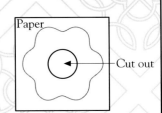

Paper

Cut out

- **To properly position the pink petals (Template #6) and gold wedges (Template #7) on the large center flowers and on the border rosebuds, make a pattern placement guide. Using a permanent marker, trace the designs on pages 111 and 112 onto a piece of clear template plastic. (Photocopying the design onto a piece of acetate is even faster!) Place the plastic over the large center flower or rosebud, matching the design lines to the appliqué. To position each small piece, lift up the plastic, slide each piece under the appropriate marking, then pin or baste the appliqué in place.**

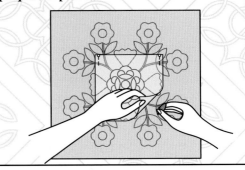

Quilt Top Assembly and Finishing

Refer to "Assembly and Finishing Techniques," beginning on page 88.

1. If you cut the background blocks oversize, trim them all to 24½" x 24½", being sure to keep the design centered in each of the 9 blocks.

2. Arrange the blocks in 3 rows of 3 blocks each. Sew the blocks together in rows. Press the seams open. Sew the rows together, being careful to match the seams. Press the seams open. (Seams of appliqué blocks made with light background fabric should be pressed open. That way, the seam allowances will show through on both sides of the seam lines for a more balanced look rather than on one side only.)

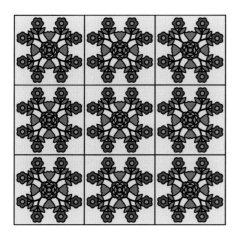

3. Sew the border strips to the edges of the quilt as shown for "Borders with Mitered Corners" on pages 90–91.

4. Trace the corner swags and flowers in each corner of the quilt. Appliqué the corner swags, piece 1a, and flower pieces 9–12, to complete the design.

5. Mark the quilting design on the quilt top. Mark the 12" Feather Wreath design (on the pullout pattern at the back of the book) in the 4 spaces where the blocks come together. Mark diagonal lines in the background. Mark the center diagonal lines first, then mark parallel lines ³/₄" apart.

6. Layer the quilt top with batting and backing; baste.
7. Outline-quilt around the appliqués. Quilt the large feather wreaths. Quilt on the marked lines.
8. Bind the edges with background fabric.
9. Add a label to your finished quilt. See page 94.

WELCOME PINEAPPLE

Quilt Dimensions: 29¹/₂" x 29¹/₂"   Block Size: 13" x 13"

*T*his Pineapple quilt in the Smithsonian collection was made in the nineteenth century. The quilt is said to have been made by the great-great-great aunt of the donor, Lenore Fallen. The Pineapple motif in the 13" blocks is reflected in the 12"-wide border of appliquéd swags with large and small pineapples.

Since colonial times, pineapples have been the symbol of welcome and hospitality. The pineapple was also used in furniture and architectural design.

The Smithsonian quilt was made with light green and light orange solid-colored cotton fabrics on a white cotton background. The striking colors are bright and very suitable for the design. It is interesting to note that one block was made with an orange cotton fabric darker than the one used in the other blocks.

I made the new quilt, a wall hanging, using the green and brown prints from the RJR Smithsonian fabrics inspired by quilts in the collection. The Pineapple block in the center is the same size as the one in the original quilt. I adapted the border from the small pineapples in the border of the original quilt. If you wish, you can make a quilt like the original by stitching 16 Pineapple blocks and referring to the photo of the original quilt for the layout. The Smithsonian quilt has patchwork in the center of the large pineapples. I adapted the directions for "Welcome Pineapple" so that the center was appliquéd instead—less work than piecing.

Make these contemporary pineapples as a "Welcome" wall hanging for your home or a special housewarming gift for a special friend.

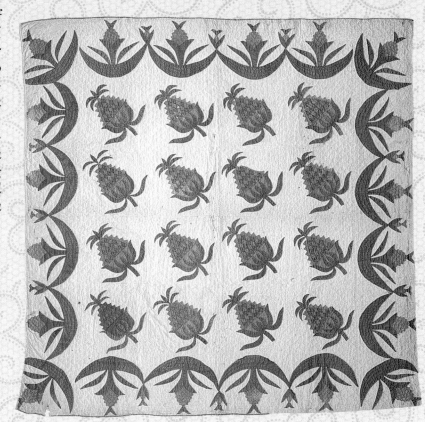

PINEAPPLE
quilt from the Smithsonian collection, 189.1cm x 195.2cm (74¹/₂" x 77").

WELCOME PINEAPPLE
by Mimi Dietrich, 1995, Baltimore, Maryland, 29¹/₂" x 29¹/₂".

Pineapple

Cutting

From the background fabric, cut:

1 square, 13¹/2" x 13¹/2", for the center block

4 strips, each 5³/4" x 32", for the border

From the gold print, cut:

4 strips, each 2" x 44", for binding

2 squares, each 10¹/2" x 10¹/2". Cut the squares once
diagonally for a total of 4 setting triangles.

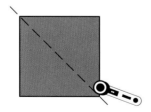

Pineapple Block Cutting and Assembly

1. Use the patterns on the pullout pattern at the back of the book to make a freezer-paper template for pieces 1–5 and 7–16 of the Pineapple block. (See "Freezer-Paper Appliqué" on pages 87–88.) You will need one freezer-paper shape for each piece. Cut out the shapes on the lines. Iron pieces 7, 8, and 9 to the *wrong* side of the gold print. Iron all other pieces to the *wrong* side of the green fabric. Cut out each shape ¹/4" outside of the paper edges.

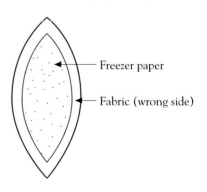

Freezer paper

Fabric (wrong side)

2. Trace the Pineapple center (piece 6 on the pullout pattern) onto freezer paper. Referring to the illustration below, carefully mark each section with the appropriate letter and color. Cut the pineapple center apart on the lines. Separate the pieces into two piles, one for green, the other for gold. Iron the appropriate pieces to the *right* side of the green and gold fabrics. Cut out each section 1/4" away from the outer edge of the freezer-paper shape.

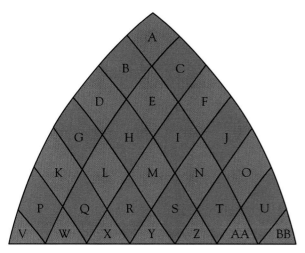

Pattern Placement Guide

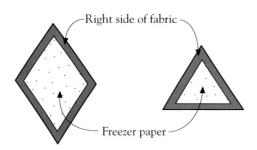

3. Center and trace the pineapple design onto the 13 1/2" square of background fabric.

4. Appliqué leaves 1–5 at the top of the pineapple. The base of leaves 1 and 2 will be covered by the center; leaves 3 and 4 will be covered by leaf 5.

5. Appliqué the pineapple, piece by piece, beginning at the top. Referring to "Appliqué with Freezer Paper on Top" on page 88, appliqué gold piece A over the raw edges at the bottom of the leaves. Appliqué the top adjacent edges of A only. The bottom edges should lie flat and will be covered by the next row of pieces. Remove the freezer paper.

6. Appliqué green pieces B and C over the bottom edge of piece A. The bottom and side edges should lie flat and will be covered by the next row and the side pineapple pieces. See the Tip on page 62 to make positioning the pieces easy.

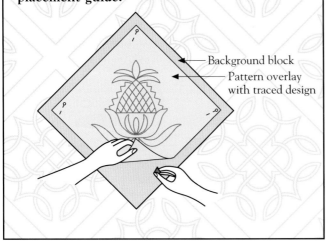
7. Continue adding pieces in alphabetical order until the diamond area is completed.
8. Appliqué the gold pieces 7, 8, and 9 over the raw edges of the pineapple center.

9. Appliqué the bottom leaves in numerical order. Set the completed block aside.

Pineapple Border

1. Using the border design on the pullout pattern at the back of the book, make a freezer-paper template for each piece. Place the coated side of the shapes on the wrong side of the appropriate fabrics and iron in place with a warm, dry iron. Cut 1/4" from the outer edges of each freezer-paper shape. Cut 20 pineapples (Template #3) from gold fabric. Cut the following pieces from the green fabric.

   16 side swags (Template #1)
   20 pineapple tops (Template #2)
   20 leaves (Template #4)
   20 leaves (Template #4r)
   4 corner swags (Template #5)

2. Fold each border strip in half to find the center. Place the center fold over the center marking on the border pattern. Trace the small pineapples and side swags on the background fabric.

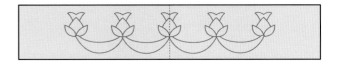

3. Appliqué the side swags and 3 center pineapples to each border strip in numerical order. Refer to "Freezer-Paper Appliqué" on pages 87–88. *Do not appliqué the outer pineapples or corners yet.*

Quilt Top Assembly and Finishing

Refer to "Assembly and Finishing Techniques," beginning on page 88.

1. Sew a large setting triangle to opposite sides of the Pineapple block as shown, then add setting triangles to the remaining sides. Press the seams toward the center block.

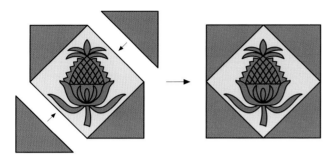

2. Sew the border strips to the edges of the quilt, following the directions for "Borders with Mitered Corners" on pages 90–91.

3. Trace the corner swags on each border corner. Appliqué the swags and then the remaining pineapples in place.

4. Mark the quilting design on the quilt top. The original quilt had an allover Clamshell design. This was used in the center of the new quilt around the pineapple. The design appears on page 110. Referring to the border design, mark quilting lines on the border. Do not mark quilting over the appliqué pieces in the border.

5. Layer the quilt top with batting and backing; baste.
6. Outline-quilt around the appliqués. Quilt on the marked lines.
7. Bind the edges with gold print binding.
8. Add a label to your finished quilt. See page 94.

LILIES OF THE QUILTERS

Quilt Dimensions: 78¹/2" x 89³/4" ❧ Block Size: 8" x 8"

The Lily quilt is an album of red-and-green pieced Lily blocks signed by many quilters from Emmitsburg, Taneytown, and Westminster, Maryland. These towns are west of Baltimore, where more elaborate red-and-green album quilts were made in the mid-nineteenth century. Thirty-seven of the blocks are signed in ink, and two in cross-stitch. The quilt is dated 1843–1845 and is said to have belonged to Pink Phillips, mother of Miss Marion Taylor, the donor of the quilt.

The Lily block design was popular during the nineteenth century. It is often referred to as the Peony, Cactus Flower, or Tulip.

My friends and students used contemporary fabrics to make the Lily blocks for a new quilt. The size of the new quilt was determined by the number of blocks I received. There were enough for two new quilts, each with forty-two Lily blocks. It is amazing to me that with so many hands at work, only three red fabrics were repeated in the total of eighty-four blocks! Most of the blocks were pieced by hand, a few by machine. Many of my students appliquéd the entire block design because it is their favorite method of quiltmaking. They basted fabric over freezer-paper shapes, stitched the flower petals together, then appliquéd them to the background.

This quilt block is fun to make because it is a combination of patchwork and appliqué. You can make your quilt using scraps, or choose a favorite red fabric and a favorite green one. This would be a great project to record the members of your quilt guild.

LILY
quilt from the Smithsonian collection, 258.4cm x 264.2cm (101⁷/8" x 103⁷/8").

LILIES OF THE QUILTERS
by students and friends of
Mimi Dietrich, 1994, Baltimore, Maryland,
78¹/₂" x 89³/₄". Quilted by Amish friends.

MATERIALS: 44"-WIDE FABRIC

1½ yds. assorted reds for flowers

1¾ yds. assorted greens
for stems and leaves

3 yds. assorted off-white fabrics for
background in pieced blocks

3¼ yds. off-white for
setting squares and triangles

2⅜ yds. red for inner border

2⅝ yds. green for outer border

5½ yds. coordinating fabric for backing

1 yd. green for binding

83" x 94" piece of batting

Thread

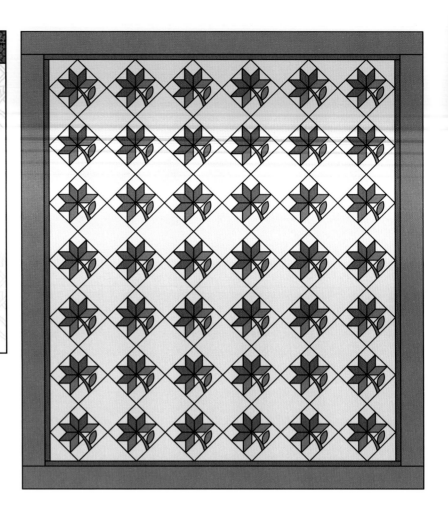

Lily

Lilies of the Quilters Quilt-Block Stitchers

Carol Allison
Mary Anderson
Pat Bailey
Peggy Bonner
Susan Brunt
Sandra Bryant
Pamela Budesheim
Rosemary Bull
Ann Christy
Betty Jo Clark
Kitty Kelly Corbitt
Helen Collins
Anne Connery
Frances Costas
Joan Costello
Dolores Dallas
Candy Davis
Roslyn Dial
Betty Diggs
Eleanor Eckman
Regina English

Pauline Erb
Brenda Finnegan
Carol Forsbeck
Christine Frost
Lois Gant
Julianne Hardy
Lucille Herber
Phyllis Hess
Judy Hilliard
Joan Hinkley
Dorothy Hunt
Thelma Hunter
Lynn Irwin
Jean Itzel
Helen Johnston
Elisabeth Kershaw
Betty Klabunde
Joan Kuczka
Eleanor Layman
Daisy Lerner
Alice Lynch

Carol MacPhail
Pat Mayes
Jennifer Mayrovitz
Marylou McDonald
Barbara McMahon
June McMurry
Vickie Messent
Chris Miller
June Mitchell
Betty Morton
Pat Mueller
Leona Pancoast
Marian Price
Judy Purman
Trish Raidt
Barbara Rasch
Nora Reedy
Jean Reger
Debra Reynolds
Karen Ringrose
Mary Rivard

Robbyn Robinson
Mary Beth Rose
Karen Ruthig
Mary Rutter
Jody Schatz
Dori Sharon
Peggie Shedd
Leda Sierer
Kay Smith
Kathleen Smith
Millie Tracey
Mary Stewart
Phyllis Van Meerhaeghe
Carolyn Walters
Lea Wang
Constance Waxter
Phyllis Wilkinson
Jackie Wilcox

Cutting

Use the templates on page 113. Templates #5 and #6 are for appliqué,. Refer to the template-making directions for appliqué, beginning on page 83.

From the assorted red fabrics for the blocks, cut:
168 Template #1

From the assorted green fabrics for the blocks, cut:
84 Template #1

42 appliqué Template #5

42 appliqué Template #6

From the assorted off-white background fabric for pieced blocks, cut:
168 Template #2

84 Template #3

42 Template #4

From the off-white background fabric for setting squares and triangles, cut:
30 squares, each 8½" x 8½", for the alternate setting squares

6 squares, each 12³/₈" x 12³/₈". Cut the squares twice diagonally for a total of 24 side setting triangles. There are 2 extra triangles.

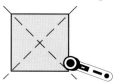

2 squares, 6½" x 6½". Cut the squares once diagonally for a total of 4 corner setting triangles.

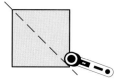

From the red border fabric, cut:
4 strips, each 1½" wide and the length of the fabric, for the inner border

From the green border fabric, cut:
4 strips, each 5" wide and the length of the fabric, for the outer border

Lily Block Assembly

1. Arrange the pieces for each of the 42 blocks, using 4 diamonds (Template #1) of the same fabric to create the flower for each block.

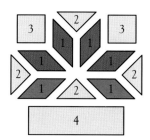

2. Sew 2 green diamonds (Template #1) to each off-white background triangle (Template #2).

Make 42

3. Add an off-white background rectangle (Template #4) to each unit from step 2.

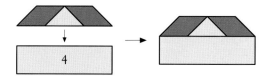

4. Appliqué the green stem (Template #5) and leaf (Template #6). See "Appliqué" on page 83.

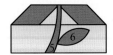
Block bottom

5. Sew 4 red diamonds (Template #1) together for each block. Begin and end all stitching at the seam intersections.

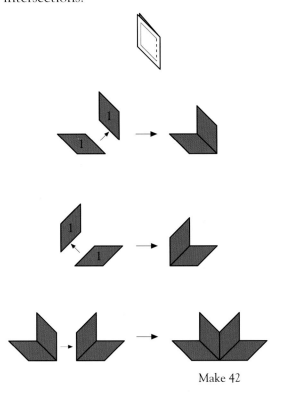
Make 42

6. Sew a red diamond unit to the bottom section of each block.

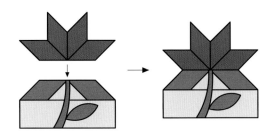

7. Add background triangles (Template #2) and squares (Template #3) to complete each block.

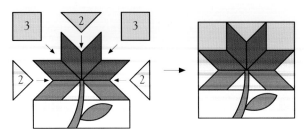

8. Sign your block using a fine-line permanent pen. Iron a piece of freezer paper to the wrong side of the block under the area where you wish to sign to keep the fabric from stretching while you write.

Quilt Top Assembly and Finishing

Refer to "Assembly and Finishing Techniques," beginning on page 88.

1. Arrange the pieced blocks, the off-white setting blocks, and the side and corner setting triangles in diagonal rows as shown. Sew the blocks and triangles together in diagonal rows. Press the seams toward the off-white squares and triangles. Sew the rows together, adding the 2 corner triangles last.

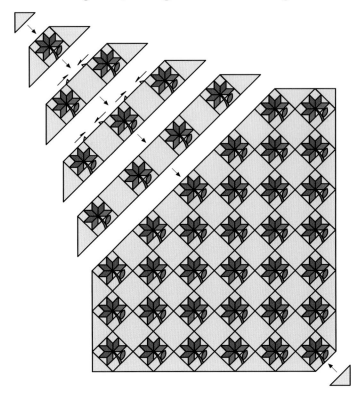

2. Sew the 1¹/₂"-wide red border strips to the sides of the quilt and press the seams toward the border. Add the top and bottom red border strips in the same manner. Follow the directions for cutting and attaching "Borders with Straight-Cut Corners" on pages 89–90.

3. Repeat step 2 with the 5"-wide green border strips.

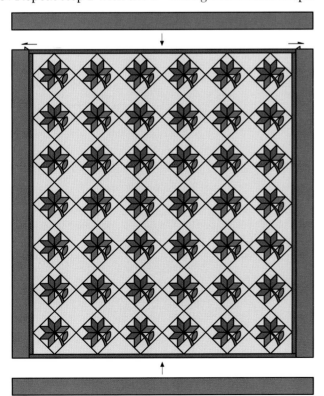

4. Mark the quilting design on the quilt top. The original quilt has an allover 1" diagonal grid. The contemporary quilt has flowers and leaves quilted in the background squares and triangles. The pattern appears on page 114. Outline quilting was done around the outer edges of the lilies and stems and inside each diamond. The border has a traditional cable pattern. Use your favorite design.

5. Layer the quilt top with batting and backing; baste.
6. Quilt on the marked lines.
7. Bind the edges with green binding.
8. Add a label to your finished quilt. See page 94.

$\mathcal{P}$INWHEELS

Quilt Dimensions: 83" x 101" ❦ Block Size: 9" x 9"

*T*his pieced Pinwheel quilt, with elaborate stuffed quilting, was made circa 1812–14 in Maryland. It was donated to the Smithsonian by Mrs. Cecil H. Naylor. The quilt is said to have been made by the women of the family while the men were away during the War of 1812. One of the women was a Mrs. Adams, great-great grandmother of the donor.

This Pinwheel pattern is based on a ninepatch grid. Five of the nine squares in the block are divided into triangles, forming the pinwheels and creating movement in the design. Ten different quilting designs were used in the plain blocks. The quilting transforms the simple pattern into a masterpiece quilt. The 8"-wide white border has a quilted and stuffed feathered vine and small floral motifs.

The original quilt was made with white solid cotton and blue-and-white and pink-and-white windowpane checked fabric. All of these tiny pieces were stitched by hand. There are a total of 2,420 pieces in the original blocks!

The new quilt was made with white cotton and five different dark blues to give variation to the pinwheels. The size of the pinwheel was changed from 1" squares to 1½" squares for ease in piecing the blocks. My friend Mary Hickey made the new quilt and I fell in love with her quick and easy technique for making the half-square triangle units that make up the Pinwheel blocks!

It's up to you—sit back, relax, and hand cut and piece the pinwheels, or oil up your machine and make this quilt with new techniques!

PINWHEEL *quilt from the Smithsonian collection, 207.4cm x 228.3cm (81³/4" x 90").*

PINWHEELS
*by Mary Hickey,1994, Seattle, Washington,
83" x 101" Quilted by Clara Hershberger.*

Template Cutting
and Hand Piecing

Note: Yardage and directions for rotary cutting and speed piecing begin on page 73.

MATERIALS: 44"-WIDE FABRIC

8¹/₂ yds. white solid for patchwork background, setting blocks, and border

1/2 yd. each of 5 different blue prints

1/8 yd. dark red fabric for one pinwheel

6 yds. white fabric for backing

1 yd. blue print for binding

87" x 105" piece of batting

Thread

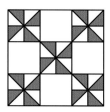

Pinwheel

Template Cutting

Use the templates on page 115.
From the white solid fabric, cut a 3-yard length.
From this piece, cut:
2 strips, each 10¹/₂" x 87", for the top
and bottom borders

2 strips, each 10¹/₂" x 105", for the side borders

From the remaining white solid fabric, cut:
640 Template #1

128 Template #2

31 setting squares, each 9¹/₂" x 9¹/₂"

From the blue prints, cut:
636 Template #1 (or 640 for all blue pinwheels)

From the dark red fabric, cut:
4 Template #1

Traditional Block Assembly

1. Sew a blue triangle (Template #1) to a white triangle along the long side to form a square. Press the seam toward the blue fabric. Repeat to make 636 blue-and-white half-square triangle units. Repeat with the 4 red triangles to make 4 red-and-white half-square triangle units.

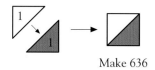

Make 636

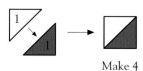

Make 4

---

2. Arrange 4 pieced squares as shown. Sew them together to form a pinwheel. Make 1 red-and-white pinwheel and 159 blue-and-white pinwheels.

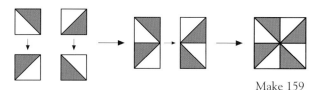

Make 159

Make 1

3. For each block, arrange 5 pinwheels and 4 white squares (Template #2) in rows as shown. Sew together in rows. Press the seams away from the white squares. Place the red-and-white pinwheel unit in the corner of one of these blocks.

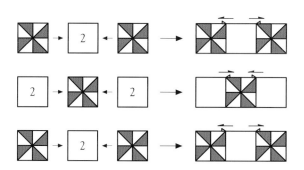

4. Sew the rows together to make a total of 32 Pinwheel blocks.

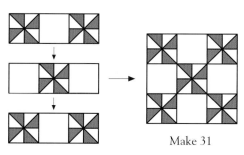

Make 31

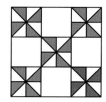

Make 1

5. See "Quilt Top Assembly and Finishing," page 76.

Rotary Cutting and Speed Piecing

All measurements include 1/4"-wide seam allowances.

Mary Hickey made the new Pinwheels quilt using the Bias Square® ruler designed by Nancy J. Martin of That Patchwork Place. The square acrylic ruler features a diagonal line to assist you in cutting half-square triangle units—pinwheels!

Mary's Pinwheels quilt contains 640 bias-square units, the name for the half-square triangle units that you create using strip piecing and the Bias Square. To make perfectly accurate bias squares in a comparatively short time, you cut bias strips of fabric, sew them together, and cut squares from the sewn strips.

MATERIALS: 44"-WIDE FABRIC

11 1/2 yds. white solid for patchwork background, setting blocks, and border

1 yd. each of 5 different blue prints

1/8 yd. dark red fabric for one pinwheel

6 yds. white fabric for backing

1 yd. blue print for binding

87" x 105" piece of batting

Thread

Rotary Cutting

From the white solid fabric, cut:
2 strips, each 10 1/2" x 87", for top and bottom borders

2 strips, each 10 1/2" x 105", for side borders

31 setting squares, each 9 1/2" x 9 1/2"

11 strips, each 3 1/2" x 42". Crosscut 128 squares, each 3 1/2" x 3 1/2".

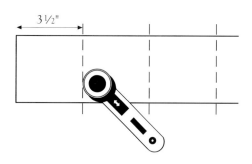

From the remaining white solid fabric, cut:
20 pieces, each approximately 18" x 22"
(also known as fat quarters)

From each blue fabric, cut:
4 pieces, each approximately 18" x 22", for a
total of 20 rectangles (fat quarters)

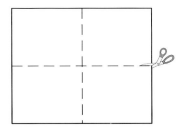

From the red fabric, cut:
2 squares, each 2³/8" x 2³/8". Cut once
diagonally for a total of 4 triangles.

Bias Square Construction

1. Layer one blue and one white rectangle with right sides facing up. You will cut strips of both colors at the same time.

2. To make the first bias cut, measure and mark 3" from the bottom left corner in both the horizontal and vertical directions. Place one edge of a 24"-long acrylic rotary-cutting ruler at these marks and cut along the right edge of the ruler.

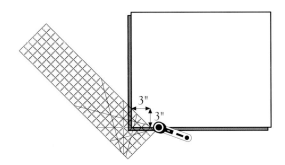

3. Align the 2" mark on your ruler with the cut edge of the fabric and cut a 2"-wide bias strip. Continue cutting 2"-wide strips in the same manner, making all cuts parallel to the first cut. Cut until you can no longer cut a 2"-wide piece.

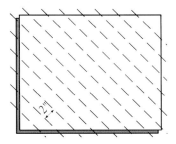

4. Separate and arrange the bias strips into 2 units, alternating blue and white in each unit. *The bottom left corner of each unit should be a different color as shown.*

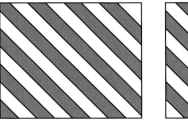 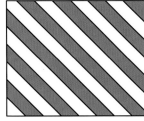

Unit 1   Unit 2

5. With right sides facing and offsetting the top edges ¹/4" as shown, sew the strips together to complete each strip-pieced unit. Be sure to stitch accurate ¹/4"-wide seams.

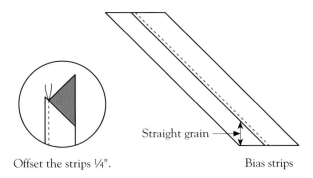

Offset the strips ¹/4".   Straight grain   Bias strips

6. Press the seams toward the blue strips. Press gently from the back of the fabric first and then on the front to make sure that the seams lie flat.

7. With the strip-pieced unit right side up, place the diagonal line of the Bias Square on one of the interior seams in the unit. Align a long cutting ruler with the edge of the Bias Square, just covering the uneven edge of the strip unit. Move the Bias Square aside and trim the edge of the unit so that it is a perfect 45° angle to the seam lines. As you trim the edge of the unit, you are actually cutting one side of many bias squares, so accurate cutting is essential.

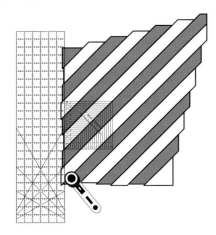

8. Align the 2" mark on the ruler with the newly cut edge and cut a strip-pieced segment from the unit. As you cut this strip, you are actually cutting the second side of many squares. Set strip aside.

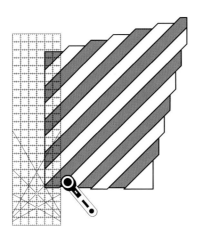

9. For continued cutting accuracy, you must trim the edge of the unit before cutting each segment (as in step 7). Continue to cut segments until you have cut up the entire unit.

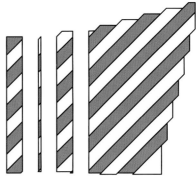

10. Use the Bias Square to cut the segments into 2" squares. Position the edge of the Bias Square at the edge of the fabric, aligning the bias line with a seam line as shown and cut along the right edge of the ruler. Continue across the remainder of the strip in the same manner. You are cutting the third side of each bias square.

11. Turn the segments around. The easiest way to do this is to turn the entire cutting mat, instead of turning each piece. Reposition the Bias Square with the edge of the ruler on the edge of the fabric and the diagonal line on the seam line. Trim the pieces to perfect squares.

12. Repeat steps 1–11 with the remaining fabric rectangles, cutting until you have a total of 640 bias squares.

Block Assembly

*Assemble the Pinwheel blocks,
following steps 2–4 in the directions for
"Traditional Block Assembly" on page 73.*

Quilt Top Assembly and Finishing

*Refer to "Assembly and Finishing
Techniques," beginning on page 88.*

1. Arrange the pieced blocks and the white setting squares as shown.

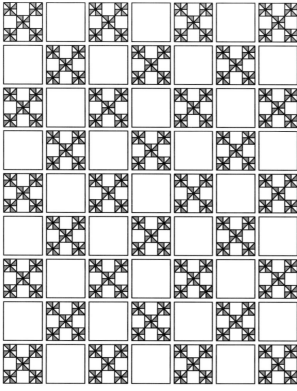

2. Sew the blocks together in rows. Press the seams toward the white setting blocks.

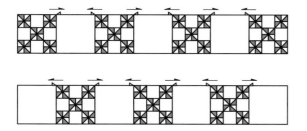

3. Sew the rows together to complete the quilt top.
4. Sew the border strips to the edges of the quilt as described for "Borders with Mitered Corners" on pages 90–91.
5. Mark the quilting design on the quilt top. The original quilt has different designs in each setting block. I have included two designs for the setting blocks, four designs for the small patchwork blocks, and a feather design for the border, on pages 115–19.
6. Layer the quilt top with batting and backing; baste.
7. Quilt on the marked lines. Outline-quilt each pinwheel.
8. Bind the edges with blue print binding.
9. Add a label to your finished quilt. See page 94.

Quiltmaking Basics for Patchwork and Appliqué

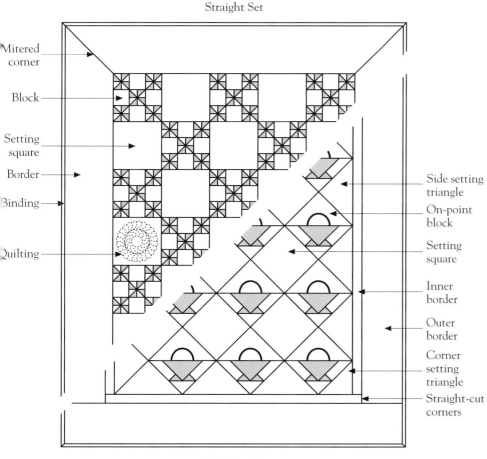

Straight Set

Mitered corner

Block

Setting square

Border

Binding

Quilting

Side setting triangle

On-point block

Setting square

Inner border

Outer border

Corner setting triangle

Straight-cut corners

On-Point Set

Fabrics for Patchwork Quilts

As you select fabrics for a pieced quilt, remember that using an assortment of solids and prints adds interest and variety to your quilt design. Choose prints that provide a mixture of pattern designs, including large floral prints, medium geometric designs, and small calico flowers.

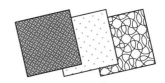

Use fabrics with similar colors and prints to give subtle shading to your quilt. Choose fabrics with light and dark color variations to accent the patchwork shapes that emerge in the quilt when blocks are combined.

Some quilt patterns can be made of fabric scraps. If you have access to scraps, feel free to use them for the designs. However, if you need to purchase fabric, yardage amounts (usually 1/8 yard) are also provided in the materials list for each quilt pattern.

FABRIC SELECTION AND PREPARATION

Most quilters like to use all-cotton fabrics because they hold their shape and are easy to handle. Quilt pieces cut from cottons blended with polyester or other fibers may tend to slip, slide, or unravel as you sew them together. Sometimes, however, the "perfect" fabric is worth a little extra care as you sew it into your quilt. Your enjoyment as you stitch the pretty colors into your design will outweigh the extra attention that may be necessary to control the fabric.

Fabrics for Appliqué Quilts

When choosing fabric for appliqué, you need fabric for two purposes: the background fabric and the appliqué pieces. Background fabrics are usually solid light colors or small prints and stripes that complement the appliqué design. White-on-white printed fabrics make lovely appliqué backgrounds. Using a bold print, plaid, or stripe as the background fabric may make it difficult to see the appliquéd design.

Fabrics used for the appliqué pieces should be appropriate for the design. Consider the proper color and print size for the pattern you are stitching. Solid fabrics are always "safe" to use, but printed fabrics can make your design more exciting. Little floral prints and geometric calicoes work well. Fabrics printed in shades of one color can be very effective for representing texture in flowers, leaves, and other natural shapes. Large multicolored prints may be too elaborate for small appliqué pieces. The design in a large print gets lost in a small appliqué piece, although sometimes you can cut a perfect design from a specific area of the large print. Avoid stripes and plaids unless they work well with your design.

Preparation

Prewash all fabrics to prevent shrinking and bleeding in the quilt. Wash dark and light colors separately with laundry detergent so that the dark colors do not run onto the light colors. Sometimes it is necessary to rinse dark fabrics a few times until the color stops bleeding and the rinse water is clear. Iron the fabrics to remove all wrinkles so that you can cut accurate pieces.

Batting

In addition to the fabric for your quilt, you will need to choose an appropriate batting for the filling between the completed quilt top and the backing fabric. Batting is available in 100% cotton, 100% polyester, or in a poly/cotton blend. The Smithsonian quilts that inspired the new quilts in this book were made with cotton batting or, in some cases, no batting at all. To maintain the feeling of antique quilts, choose a thin batting. The new light polyester battings are easy to use and launder well. A thin layer of batting makes hand quilting a delight!

TOOLS AND SUPPLIES

Thread

Be sure to use a strong thread. All-purpose cotton or cotton-covered polyester thread is sturdy and comes in a variety of colors. Use special quilting thread only for the quilting process. It is thicker than all-purpose thread and will show if you use it for piecing or appliqué.

Use thread that matches the color of your work. For machine piecing, choose a thread that blends with the predominant color in your fabrics. When hand piecing, try to match the color perfectly to the fabric so that your stitches will be invisible. When you sew together two patches of different colors, match the color of the thread to the darker fabric. Match the color of the solid fabric if one is a print and one is a solid. When using two prints, use a color that is repeated in both prints so that it blends with both. When sewing by hand, use a thread length no longer than 18" to avoid tangles and to prevent it from wearing as it is drawn through the fabric over and over as you work.

Thread for appliqué should match the color of the appliqué pieces rather than the background fabric. Designs with many different-colored pieces require many shades of thread. If it is not possible to match the color exactly, choose thread that is a little darker than the fabric. If the appliqué fabric contains many colors, choose a neutral-colored thread that blends with the predominant color.

All-cotton thread works well for stitching appliqués. It is pliable and disappears or blends invisibly into the edges of the appliqués. If cotton thread is not available in just the right color, use cotton-covered polyester thread. Sometimes it's necessary to use thread that you have available at that moment in your sewing area. If so, make sure that the thread is strong and that it is a close color match to your appliqué pieces.

Always use light-colored thread for basting, since dye from dark thread often leaves behind small dots of color on light fabrics.

Needles and Pins

A fine needle (sizes 8 to 12) glides easily through your fabric as you piece by hand. Choose the smallest-size needle that you can easily thread. Betweens (quilting needles) are short and will help you feel close to your work. For more information on Betweens, refer to "Quilting Supplies" on page 92. Longer needles (Sharps) are often easier for some stitchers to control and enable you to gather more stitches on them as you sew. Long needles with large eyes (crewels) are easier to thread. An even longer type of needle (milliner's) works well as a tool for "needle-turning" the appliqué edge as it is applied to the background. Try different types of needles and you will soon find the one most comfortable for you. If a thin needle is difficult to thread, use a needle threader.

Quilting needle (Between)

Sharp

Crewel

Milliner's

For machine-stitched patchwork, a fine needle (size 10/70) sews through fabric easily. For heavier fabrics, use size 12/80.

When you choose a needle for appliqué, the most important consideration is the size of the needle. A thin needle glides easily through the edges of the appliqué pieces, making it easy to create small stitches and helping your thread to blend into the fabrics. Size 10 (fine) to size 12 (very fine) needles work well.

Long "quilter's pins" with glass or plastic heads are easy to handle when sewing patchwork. Small 3/4" sequin pins are wonderful for pin-basting appliqué pieces.

Scissors

Use your best and sharpest scissors to cut fabric, saving an older pair for cutting paper, cardboard, or template plastic. Small 4" scissors are great for clipping patchwork threads and appliqués.

Template Materials

Sheets of clear or frosted plastic are available at quilt shops. This material is an excellent choice for making durable, accurate templates (stiff pattern pieces). It is easy to mark plastic templates with a fine-line permanent marking pen. Be sure to mark the grain-line arrow, the letter, and the name of the quilt on the template for accurate placement on the fabric and easy identification. You can also make templates by tracing the appropriate pattern shapes onto paper, then gluing the paper to cardboard and cutting out the shapes. These may not last as long as plastic templates.

To keep a template from slipping and sliding while you trace around it on your fabric, place a piece of double-sided tape on the underside of the template. Some quilters prefer to attach small circles of sandpaper instead. Another alternative is to place a sheet of fine sandpaper under your fabric to keep it from slipping while you work.

Marking Pencils

To ensure accuracy, templates must be traced from the book and then traced onto fabric with a marking tool that produces a sharp, fine line. To trace templates onto fabric, use a regular pencil (#2 or #3) or a fine-lead (.5mm) mechanical pencil that will remain sharp through many markings. Silver marking pencils, available in most quilt shops, work well on very light and very dark fabrics. A chalk pencil makes clear marks on dark fabric. A water-erasable

marker produces a wider line that may lead to cutting and stitching inaccuracy. For more information on marking tools, refer to "Marking the Quilting Design" on page 91.

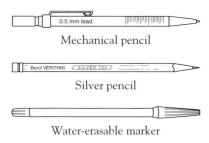

Mechanical pencil

Silver pencil

Water-erasable marker

Rulers

Clear plastic or acrylic rulers with parallel markings are essential for measuring templates, adding seam allowances, and rotary cutting straight lines.

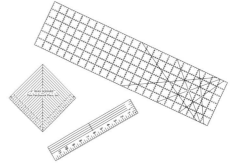

Rotary-Cutting Equipment

Many contemporary quiltmakers have traded in templates and scissors for a rotary cutter, mat, and a clear acrylic ruler. They prefer this cutting alternative for its speed and accuracy when cutting geometric patchwork shapes.

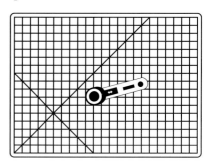

PATCHWORK BASICS

You may hand or machine piece your patchwork pieces together. Each method requires special template preparation and stitching techniques.

Hand Piecing

You can enjoy hand piecing anytime and anywhere. You can keep a few pieces in a small bag for travel and save larger pieces to work on at home. It's peaceful to stitch a quilt by hand and savor the time spent with your favorite fabrics. In traditional quiltmaking, templates and scissors are used to cut patchwork pieces for hand piecing.

MAKING HAND-PIECING TEMPLATES

For hand piecing, templates should be the same size as the finished patchwork pieces. Make templates for hand piecing by tracing the pattern pieces onto a sheet of clear plastic. The piecing templates in this book include 1/4"-wide seam allowances. If you plan to machine piece, trace the outer cutting line. However, for hand piecing, use a pencil or fine-line permanent marker to trace the pieces accurately along the design lines (dashed stitching lines), *not the outer cutting line*. Cut carefully on the lines. Do not add seam allowances.

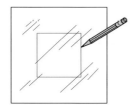

Trace pattern
onto clear plastic.

Mark the pattern name and grainline arrow on each template. This line is necessary for aligning the template on your fabric. Match the grainline arrow with the straight threads in your fabric (crosswise or lengthwise). The grain line is usually parallel to the longest side of the piece. On a right triangle, the grain line usually follows one side of the right angle. Patchwork pieces that are positioned on the outside edge of the quilt should be cut so the grain line in each piece is parallel to the quilt edge to prevent stretching.

MARKING AND CUTTING FABRIC

1. Place hand-piecing templates face down on the wrong side of your fabric. Position them so that the grain line matches the straight threads in your fabric.

Align grain line on fabric.

2. Trace around the template to mark the stitching line on the wrong side of the fabric. When tracing several pieces on your fabric, *leave at least 1/2" between tracings*.

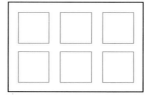

Trace around template.

3. Next, add a 1/4"-wide seam allowance all the way around each traced shape. This seam-allowance width is standard for hand and machine piecing. Use a clear acrylic ruler with parallel lines and place the 1/4" line on the marked line. With a sharp pencil, draw along the edge of the ruler to add the seam allowance. The outer marked line is the cutting line.

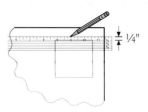

4. Carefully cut out the patchwork pieces on the cutting lines you just marked.

TIP

You may use an alternate method for quick-cutting pieces for hand piecing, using a rotary cutter, cutting mat, and an acrylic ruler marked with parallel lines. For example, if your hand-piecing template measures 2" square, the fabric piece will be 2½" square after adding seam allowances.

To rotary cut 2½" squares, cut 2½"-wide strips of fabric with the rotary cutter. Then cut across the strips every 2½" inches. After cutting, place the squares on a piece of sandpaper so they will not slide. Center the template on the wrong side of each square and mark around its edges to mark the stitching line.

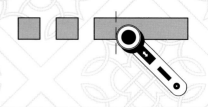

HAND STITCHING PATCHWORK PIECES

To determine what your finished quilt will look like, lay out the patchwork pieces on a flat surface. Take a minute to think about how you will stitch the pieces together. Plan to piece small units together, making larger units that you can stitch together in rows or blocks.

To sew two patches together:

1. Position the patches with right sides together and raw edges even. To fit the edges precisely, first place a pin through one corner at the point where the marked seam lines intersect. Turn the pieces over and carefully continue to stick the same pin through the seam-line corner of the matching patch. Line up the seams accurately and fasten the pin. Repeat this process at the other end of the seam. This aligns the seam line perfectly, making it easy to insert other pins along the seam.

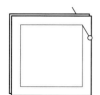

2. To sew the seam, use a single length of thread no longer than 18". Tie one knot in the end of the thread. In hand piecing, stitches begin and end at the marked seam line. *Do not take stitches in the seam allowances.*

    Insert the needle at the seam line and take a stitch. Take a backstitch in the same spot, to anchor the thread. As you make your first few stitches, move the thread tail over the seam line and catch the tail in your stitches as you sew.

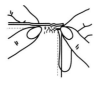 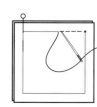

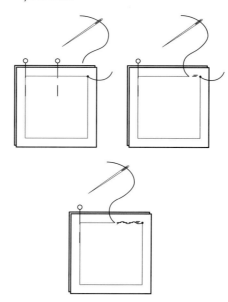

TIP

If you find that your knot pops through the first stitch, insert the needle to start stitching 3/8" in from the corner, stitch back to the corner, then stitch the entire seam.

3. Take several small running stitches on the needle, sewing the two layers together. Frequently check the other side to make sure that the stitches are following the seam line. About every inch, sew a backstitch to secure your seam.

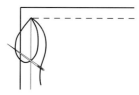

4. At the end of the seam, fasten the thread by taking a backstitch over the last stitch. Then take a small stitch in the seam allowance, pulling the needle through the loop as you tighten the thread. Weave the thread back along the seam through the last few stitches. Cut the thread short to prevent long tails of thread from shadowing through and showing on the front of your quilt when you're finished.

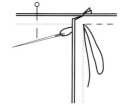

HAND PIECING ACROSS INTERSECTING SEAMS

As you sew the patches together, you will find seams that intersect each other. *Avoid sewing across the seam allowances.* As you approach an intersecting seam, make a small backstitch right before the stitching line of the seam allowance you will cross. Bring the needle and thread through the base of the seam and take another backstitch on the other side of the seam. This will keep the seam secure and accurate without catching the seam allowances in the stitches.

Pressing Seams

When the piecing is completed, press the seam allowances to one side. Finger-press the seams as you go, then press them with a steam iron when you are ready to sew the blocks together. If possible, press seams toward the darker fabric. This prevents the seam from "shadowing through" the lighter fabric and showing on the right side of the quilt. Sometimes, to make the quilting process easier, seams are pressed to one side or the other to prevent bulky areas.

If you did not stitch across seam allowances when hand piecing, you can press seams in opposing directions at the intersections to evenly distribute the thickness of the seam allowances. This also makes hand quilting easier.

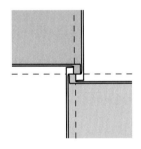

Machine Piecing

Many quilters like to use the sewing machine to assemble pieced blocks and to sew pieced and hand-appliquéd blocks together. It's also faster to use the machine to attach borders and bindings.

MAKING MACHINE-PIECING TEMPLATES

Seam allowances are included in templates for machine piecing. All piecing templates in this book include seam allowances, with the stitching line represented by dashed lines. For machine piecing, trace around the outer edges of the template shape onto template plastic and mark with the pattern name and grainline arrow. It is not necessary to mark the seam line on the templates. Cut out the template.

MARKING AND CUTTING FABRIC

1. Place the template face down on the wrong side of your fabric. Position the template so the grain line matches the straight threads in the fabric.
2. Trace around the outer edges of the template.
3. Carefully cut out the patchwork piece on the pencil line. You may use an alternate method for quick-cutting pieces as shown in the Tip on page 80.

SEWING THE PIECES TOGETHER

Stitching an accurate 1/4"-wide seam is the key to machine piecing so that all the pieces fit together precisely. Many machines have a presser foot that measures 1/4" from the needle to the outer right edge of the foot. If this is true for your machine, you should be able to guide the fabric into your machine so that the fabric edge aligns with the right edge of the foot and still obtain a seam that measures 1/4" wide.

To test your machine for seam-width accuracy, sew a seam as described above, then measure the seam allowance from the stitching to the edge of the fabric. If the measurement is not exactly 1/4", adjust in one of two ways.

If your machine has a needle-position control, you can move the needle to the left or to the right to make your seam allowance accurate. If your needle cannot be adjusted, you may have to change the way you feed the fabric into the machine.

The easiest and most accurate way to adjust your stitching is to locate the point that is exactly 1/4" from your needle and place a piece of masking tape on the bed of the machine in that location. Add a few layers of tape to create a ridge that will help you guide the fabric edges.

To machine stitch two patches together:

1. Set the machine for 12 to 15 stitches per inch.
2. Place the patches right sides together, matching the raw edges to be joined.
3. Feed the pieces into the machine, aligning the raw edges with the edge of the presser foot or the masking-tape guide. Stitch from cut edge to cut edge. It is not necessary to backstitch at either end as the seams will be crossed by others.

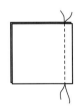

Sewing patchwork pieces together is more fun and a lot faster if you chain-piece the patches into the machine as you sew. Plus, you'll save thread.

1. *Begin by sewing the first patch as described above. At the end of the seam, stop sewing, but don't cut the thread.*

2. *Prepare the next set of patches and feed it into the machine right after the first one. Continue feeding pieces without cutting the thread.*

3. *After sewing as many sets as possible, take your chain of patches to the ironing board and press as described above. Snip the threads between the patches to free them for the next step.*

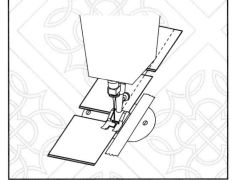

4. Press first from the back, then from the front, eliminating any pleats and flattening the seam as much as possible. Do not press seams open. Press each seam in the direction of least resistance, or toward the darker fabric. When you sew the next seam, stitch across the seam allowances.

MACHINE PIECING ACROSS INTERSECTING SEAMS

It is easier to match intersecting seams when joining two sets of patches if you plan the pressing so that the seams go in opposite directions. This reduces bulk and the seam lines nest together for easier stitching.

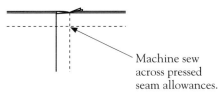

Machine sew across pressed seam allowances.

When sewing together appliqué blocks made with light background fabric, it is better to press the seams open. The seams will show through on both sides of the seam lines for a more balanced look rather than on one side only.

Press seams open between light background appliqué blocks.

APPLIQUÉ

Appliqué pieces stitched to background fabrics create beautiful designs on quilts. Instead of piecing fabric patches together to create patterns, appliqué designs are sewn to the surface of other fabrics. Appliqué is particularly appropriate and much easier than piecing for curved pieces and intricate designs.

Traditional Hand Appliqué

For the traditional appliqué method, make templates for the appliqué pieces by tracing the pattern pieces onto a sheet of clear plastic. You may also make templates by gluing paper patterns to cardboard, but plastic templates are more durable and accurate.

MAKING TEMPLATES AND CUTTING THE PIECES

1. Place the template plastic over each pattern piece and trace with a pencil or fine-line permanent marker. *Do not add seam allowances.* Cut out the templates along the traced lines so that they are the exact size of the designs. If a design is repeated in a quilt, you only need one plastic template for each design. For example, you need only one rose template to make all the roses in the Chesapeake Rose quilt shown on page 53.

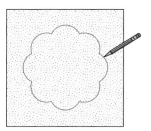

2. Place the appliqué template *right side up on the right side of the appliqué fabric*. If possible, place the templates on the appliqué fabric so that the grain runs in the same direction as the background fabric. (Appliqué designs do not usually provide grain lines to aid in placing the templates on the fabric.) Trace around the template with a sharp pencil. Place a sheet of sandpaper under the fabric to keep it from slipping or put a small piece of double-faced tape on the underside of the template. When tracing several pieces on fabric, leave at least 1/2" between tracings.

TIP

In many appliqué designs, you may want the template to match a design printed on the fabric. In this case, disregard grain lines and enjoy the way that the fabric and the appliqué design work together.

---

3. Cut out each fabric piece, adding a 1/4"-wide allowance around each tracing. This allowance will be turned under to create the finished edge of the appliqué.

MARKING THE DESIGN ON THE BACKGROUND BLOCKS

The background fabric for appliqué is usually cut in a square. If the finished size of an appliqué block is 10" square, the block must be cut 10 1/2" square to allow for seam allowances. Sometimes it is better to cut the square an inch larger to start, then trim it to the correct size after completing the appliqué. Use a large square acrylic ruler and a rotary cutter and mat to cut background squares easily and accurately.

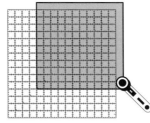

To place the appliqué pieces on the background squares accurately, mark the design on the fabric. If your background is white or off-white, it's easy to trace the design directly onto the fabric in the following manner.

Place the fabric right side up over the pattern so that the design is centered. Trace the design carefully. I like to use a silver marking pencil to trace the design. The marks are dark enough and wash out after the quilt is completed. Test the marker on a sample of your fabric to make sure you can remove the marks with cold water. Use a sharp pencil or a fine-line mechanical pencil to trace slightly inside the pattern lines so that the lines will later be covered with the placement of the appliqués.

If your background fabric is dark, work on a light box when tracing the design. If you do not have a light box, try taping the pattern to a window or storm door on a sunny day. Tape your fabric over the pattern and trace the design.

You can also create your own light box by opening your dining room table and placing a piece of glass over the table-leaf opening. Place a lamp or flashlight on the floor to shine through the glass like a light box. Place your pattern on the glass, then your fabric on top of the pattern. The light will shine through so that you can easily trace your design.

PREPARING APPLIQUÉS

Before sewing the appliqué fabrics to the background fabric, prepare the appliqués so that the seam allowances are turned under smoothly. This will help you to place the appliqués accurately on the background fabric.

1. Turn under the seam allowances, rolling the traced line to the back. Baste around each piece with light-colored thread. Try looking at the right side of the piece while you turn the edge under, basting right along the fold. This helps to keep the piece neat and accurate as you concentrate on the smooth shape of the piece. If you keep your stitches near the fold, you will be sure to catch the seam allowance.

2. If one appliqué piece overlaps another, leave edges that will be covered by other appliqué pieces unturned so they will lie flat under the overlapping pieces.

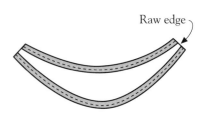

Raw edge

The heart is a perfect shape to practice basting because it contains most of the features you will find in other appliqué shapes: a straight edge, curves, an outside point, and an inside point.

1. Start to baste the heart along the straight edge. Leave the thread unknotted so it will be easy to remove later. Take a few stitches as you turn under the straight edge, stopping just before you reach the outside point.

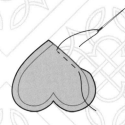

2. To prepare the outside point, first turn the point of the fabric in toward the appliqué. Fold the right side under, then the left, to form a sharp point.

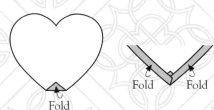

The seam allowances may overlap slightly. On a sharper point, they will overlap more. If the seam allowance is too thick, trim it or later push the extra fabric under the point with your needle as you sew. Baste close to the edge.

3. Continue basting the straight area of the heart until you come to the first curve at the top of the heart. As you baste the curve, ease the seam allowance around the curve. Do not clip the outside curve, as it will result in little bumps along the edge of the appliqué. If your seam allowance is larger than $1/4$", it helps to trim it to a "skimpy" $1/4$" around the curve ($3/16$"). As you baste around the curve, keep your basting stitches small. Sew near the fold to keep the shape accurate. If little points appear along the curve, you can push these under with the tip of your needle when you sew the appliqué to the background fabric.

4. As you finish basting the first curve, you will come to the inside point. Carefully clip the seam allowance so that the fabric will turn under easily. Stop clipping about two threads out from the marked line. As you baste the inside point, use smaller basting stitches, but do not force the threads at the point to turn under. These will be pushed under with the tip of the needle as you sew. Tack down the seam-allowance edges, taking stitches away from the inside point. This method will prevent fraying at the inside point. Baste the second curve at the top of the heart, then overlap the beginning of your basting stitches along the straight edge. Leave your basting threads unknotted so they can be removed easily.

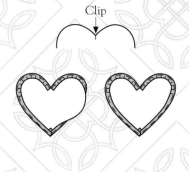

BASTING APPLIQUÉS TO THE BACKGROUND

Before appliquéing, baste the appliqué pieces to the background fabric. Most stitchers pin-baste their appliqués in place, one or two pieces at a time. Use several pins to attach the appliqué pieces to the background so that they will not slip.

Sequin pins (³/₄" long) are wonderful to use because they do not get in the way of the thread as you stitch. If you have trouble with threads tangling around pins as you sew, try placing the pins on the back side of your work, pinning from the background fabric through the appliqué pieces.

You may also hand baste the appliqué piece to the background. Use a light-colored thread, keeping the basting near the edges of the appliqués.

As an alternative to basting, position pieces and secure with water-soluble glue stick. Apply glue to the background fabric, keeping glue toward the center of the design. Glue applied on the sewing line makes the appliqué stiff and difficult to sew on the background. Place the appliqué in position and wait for it to dry before sewing. If you use a glue stick, you will need to wash the finished blocks to remove the glue.

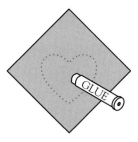

SEWING THE PIECES IN PLACE

The traditional appliqué stitch is appropriate for sewing all areas of appliqué designs, including sharp points and curves.

1. Begin with a single strand of thread approximately 18" long and tie a knot in one end. To hide your knot when you start, slip your needle into the seam allowance from the wrong side of the appliqué piece, bringing it out along the fold line. The knot will be hidden inside the seam allowance.

2. Stitch along the top edge of the appliqué. If you are right-handed, stitch from right to left. If you are left-handed, stitch from left to right. Begin the first stitch by moving your needle straight off the appliqué, inserting the needle into the background fabric.

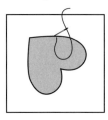

3. Move the needle under the background fabric parallel to the edge of the appliqué, bringing it up about ¹/₈" away along the pattern line. As you bring the needle back up, pierce the edge of the appliqué piece, catching only one or two threads of the folded edge.

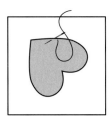

4. Move the needle straight off the appliqué into the background fabric. Move the needle under the background, bringing it up about ¹/₈" away, again catching the edge of the appliqué. Give the thread a slight tug and continue stitching. The only visible parts of the stitch are very small dots of thread along the appliqué edge. The part of the stitch that travels forward is visible as ¹/₈"-long stitches on the wrong side of the background fabric.

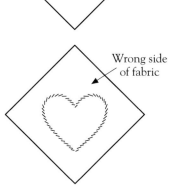

Wrong side of fabric

Note: The length of your stitches should be consistent as you stitch along the straight edges. Smaller stitches are sometimes necessary for curves and points.

5. When you get to the end of your stitching, pull your needle through to the wrong side. Behind the appliqué piece, take two small stitches, making knots by taking your needle through the loops. Before you cut the thread, take a moment to see if the threads will be shadowing through your background when you finish. If you think it will, take one more small

stitch through the back side of the appliqué to direct the tail of the thread under the appliqué fabric.

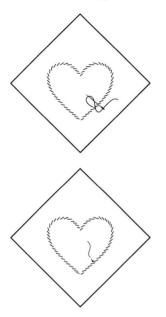

STITCHING POINTS AND CURVES

As you stitch toward an outside point, start taking smaller stitches within 1/2" of the point. If the seam allowance is too thick, trim the seam allowance or push the excess fabric under the point with the tip of your needle. Smaller stitches near the point will keep any frayed edges of the seam allowance from escaping.

Place your last stitch on the first side very close to the point. Place the next stitch on the second side of the point. A stitch on each side, close to the point, will accent the outside point. Do not make a stitch directly at the point, as it tends to flatten the point.

If a curved edge is very round, use the tip of your needle to arrange the fabric along the curve as you sew. To keep little points of fabric from sticking out, push the fabric under with the tip of your needle, smoothing the fabric along the folded edge before sewing. Keep your stitches small so those fabric points can't escape between the stitches.

On inside points, make your stitches smaller as you sew within 1/2" of the point. Stitch past the point, then return to add one extra stitch to emphasize the inside point.

Come up through the appliqué, catching a little more fabric in the inside point (four or five threads instead of one or two). Make a straight stitch outward, going under the point to pull it in a little and emphasize the shape of the inside point.

If an inside point frays, a few small close stitches will tack the fabric down securely. If your thread matches your appliqué fabric, these stitches will blend in with the edge of the shape.

Freezer-Paper Appliqué

Instead of the traditional appliqué method, you can use freezer-paper templates to help you make perfectly shaped appliqués. This technique was used to make the Chesapeake Rose quilt on page 53 and the Spring Tulips wall hanging shown on page 41.

1. Place the freezer paper, plastic-coated side down, on your pattern and trace the design with a sharp pencil. With repeated designs, such as the rose and leaves, make a plastic template and trace around it onto the freezer paper to make a freezer-paper template for each piece you need.

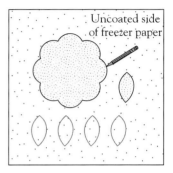

Uncoated side of freezer paper

2. Carefully cut out the freezer-paper shape on the pencil line. *Do not add seam allowances.*

3. Place the coated side of the freezer paper against the wrong side of the appliqué fabric. Iron the freezer paper to the wrong side of the appliqué fabric, using a dry, hot iron.

Wrong side of fabric

4. Cut out the appliqué shape, adding a 1/4"-wide seam allowance beyond the freezer paper's edge.

5. Turn and baste the seam allowance over the freezer-paper edges. Clip any inside points and fold outside points.

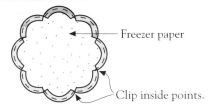
Freezer paper

Clip inside points.

6. Pin or baste the appliqué to the background fabric and stitch in place as shown for traditional appliqué.

7. After the shape has been appliquéd, remove any basting stitches. Cut a small slit in the background fabric behind the appliqué and remove the freezer paper with tweezers.

8. Press appliqué from the wrong side.

APPLIQUÉ WITH FREEZER PAPER ON TOP

This variation of the freezer-paper method was used to stitch the "All-American Eagle" medallion quilt shown on page 46.

1. Trace the design onto the uncoated side of the freezer paper and cut out on the pencil line. Iron the freezer paper to the *right* side of the appliqué fabric.

2. Cut out the appliqué shape, adding a 1/4"-wide seam allowance around the outside of the freezer paper.

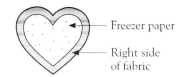
Freezer paper

Right side of fabric

3. Securely baste or pin the appliqué to the background fabric as shown for the traditional appliqué method.

4. Starting on a straight edge, use the tip of your needle to gently turn under the seam allowance. Following the shape of the paper, turn under the seam allowance so the fabric is folded at the edge of the freezer paper. Use the tip of the needle to smooth the fabric along the edge, then stitch the appliqué to the background fabric.

5. Peel away the freezer paper.

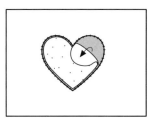

After completing your pieced or appliquéd blocks, it is time to assemble the quilt top, then layer it with batting and backing, quilt it, and bind the edges. Follow the techniques included here to make easy work of the process.

Squaring Up Blocks

Before you stitch your blocks together to assemble your quilt, it is sometimes necessary to "square up" your blocks. Trim the edges, using an acrylic ruler and rotary cutter. Be sure to leave 1/4"-wide seam allowances beyond any points or other important block details near the outer edges of the blocks.

If you cut the appliqué background squares larger than necessary, trim the blocks to the appropriate size, remembering to allow 1/4" all around for seam allowances. To make sure that the appliqué design is centered on the background, cut a square of template plastic the correct size and mark the vertical and horizontal center lines on the plastic. Center the template on the block and draw around the edges of the plastic to indicate the size; cut with scissors or a rotary cutter.

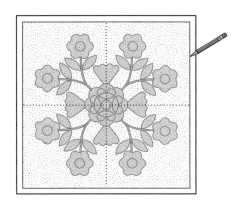

Setting the Blocks Together

Quilt blocks are sewn together in either a straight or on-point (diagonal) setting. In straight settings, blocks are laid out in rows with their straight edges parallel to the edges of the quilt.

To create a straight setting with your blocks:

1. Arrange the blocks in rows, following the quilt plan or as desired.
2. Sew the blocks together in straight horizontal or vertical rows. Press the seams in opposite directions from row to row.
3. Being careful to match seam intersections, join the rows to complete the patterned area of the quilt.

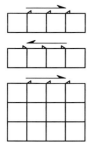

Quilts that have blocks set on point are constructed in diagonal rows, with setting triangles added to complete the corners and sides of the quilt.

To set blocks on point:

1. Lay out all the blocks and setting triangles on a flat surface before you start sewing. Arrange the pieces in diagonal rows.
2. Pick up and sew together the blocks and setting triangles in one diagonal row at a time. Press seams in opposite directions, row to row.

3. Join the rows together to complete the quilt, adding corner triangles last.

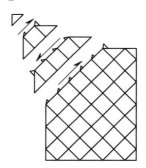

Assembly and Pressing Diagram for On-Point Set

TIP

To avoid problems with an on-point setting, make sure that all blocks are the same size and absolutely square. Plain alternate blocks must be exactly the same size as the pieced or appliquéd blocks.

Adding Borders

After setting the blocks, add the borders to frame the design. The most common borders have either straight-cut or mitered corners.

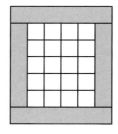

Straight-Cut Corners

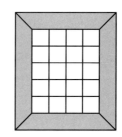

Mitered Corners

BORDERS WITH STRAIGHT-CUT CORNERS

Straight-cut borders have two of the border strips cut the length of the patchwork design and sewn to opposite sides of the quilt top. The remaining border strips are cut the total length of the resulting piece and added to the quilt top. When straight-cut borders are used in this book, the measurements reflect these dimensions.

If you are making a large quilt or a quilt with many patchwork pieces, the size of the quilt can change slightly because of all the seams involved. For this reason, it's always a good idea to cut the borders to match the actual measurements of your quilt, rather than cutting them to the exact dimensions given in the pattern you are following.

1. Measure the quilt length through the center of the patchwork. Sometimes the edges stretch, and a measurement of the center is more accurate. Using this measurement helps avoid stretched or rippled borders. Cut two border strips that match the center measurement in length and are the required width.

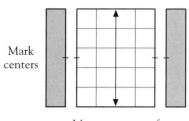

Mark centers

Measure center of quilt, top to bottom.

2. Matching outer edges and centers, pin and stitch the border strips to opposite edges of the quilt top, easing the edge of the quilt to fit the border as needed. Press the seams toward the borders.

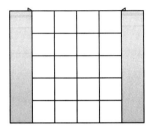

3. Measure the quilt width through the center and cut two border strips to match. Stitch to the top and bottom edges of the quilt top. Press the seams toward the borders.

Measure center of quilt, side to side, including borders.

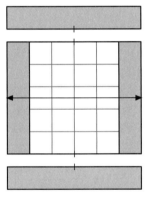

Mark centers

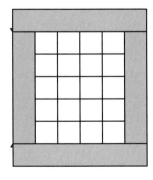

BORDERS WITH MITERED CORNERS

Mitered borders are not as difficult to add as they may look. They are especially appropriate when using a striped fabric or when adding multiple borders. Careful seam matching at the mitered corner is essential for the best results.

1. As with straight-cut borders, determine the required border length by measuring the center of the quilt.

2. Estimate the finished *outside* dimensions of your quilt, including borders. Cut each border strip at least 1" longer than the required total length.

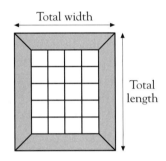

Total width

Total length

3. Fold each border strip in half crosswise and mark the center fold with a pin. Mark each edge of the quilt top in the same manner. Measure one-half of the center measurement of the quilt top from the center mark on each half of each border strip and mark with a pin. Pin-mark the quilt-top edges in the same manner. You will match the pins on the border strips to the pins on the quilt edges.

Center of border strip

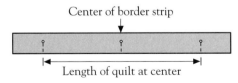

Length of quilt at center

4. With the outer pins at the raw edges of the quilt top and the centers matching, pin and sew each border to the edges of the quilt. Begin and end stitching 1/4" from the raw edges of the quilt top. Press seams toward the borders.

1/4" from quilt corner   1/4" from quilt corner

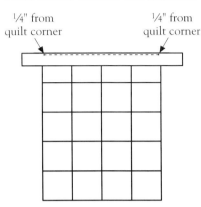

5. To miter the corners, lay a corner of the quilt top on your ironing board, pinning as necessary to keep the quilt from pulling and the corner from slipping. Fold one of the border strips under at a 45° angle. Place pins at the fold. Place a square ruler over the corner to check that the corner is flat and square. When everything is straight and square, press the fold.

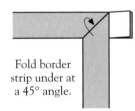

Fold border strip under at a 45° angle.

6. Carefully center a piece of 1" masking tape over the mitered fold. Remove the pins as you apply the tape.

Remove pins as you tape corner.

7. Unpin the quilt from the ironing board and turn it over. Draw a light pencil line on the crease created when you pressed the fold. Fold the center section of the quilt diagonally from the corner, right sides together, and align the long edges of the border strips. Stitch on the pencil line. Remove the tape. Check to make sure the borders lie flat, then cut away the excess fabric, leaving a 1/4"-wide seam allowance. Press the seam open. Repeat with the remaining corners.

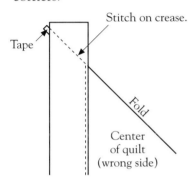

Marking the Quilting Design

Mark quilting patterns on the completed quilt top before layering and basting the quilt top with batting and backing. That way, the lines will be smooth and accurate.

There are several tools appropriate for marking the quilting design onto the quilt top. You can use a regular pencil (#2–#3), a fine-lead mechanical pencil, a silver marking pencil, or a chalk pencil or chalk marker for dark fabrics. A water-erasable marker can be used to mark the quilting design but may disappear before the quilting is completed if the weather is humid. The cleanest method for marking a dark fabric is to use a thin sliver of soap.

Whichever method you choose, test the marking tool on a sample of your fabric before using it on your quilt. Make sure you can see the lines and make sure you can remove them.

Mark straight lines by drawing along the edge of a yardstick or long, clear acrylic ruler. Parallel lines on the acrylic rulers help to keep the lines even. You can also mark straight lines with 1/4"-wide masking or quilting tape, available in quilt shops. Place the tape so that one edge is next to a seam. Then quilt along the other edge of the tape. The tape is flexible and does not interfere with the quilting process. Use wider masking tape to mark wider-spaced parallel lines for quilting. Quilt along both sides of the tape. Remove the tape and replace it to the side of the line that has been stitched. This will give you a new line to quilt that is even and parallel with the other lines.

Mark complex quilting designs by tracing patterns onto the fabric. Use a light box or tape your work against a bright window if you have trouble seeing the design through the fabric.

A wide variety of precut plastic quilting stencils is also available at quilt shops. You can make your own by tracing a quilting design on clear plastic. Cut out the lines with a double-bladed craft knife, leaving "bridges" every inch or two so the stencil will hold its shape.

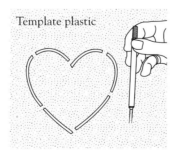

Template plastic

It may not be necessary to mark quilting designs if you are planning to quilt in-the-ditch next to seams or if you are outlining patchwork pieces.

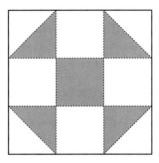

Quilting in-the-Ditch

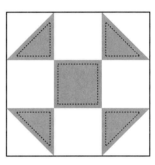

Outline Quilting

Layering and Basting

Before you begin to quilt, baste the top, batting, and backing of the quilt together. This secures the layers and keeps the fabrics from slipping.

Press the quilt backing so that it is smooth. If you need to piece the backing, trim off all selvages, sew the pieces together using 1/4"-wide seams, and press them open. The backing should be at least 2" larger than the quilt top all the way around. Place the backing on a smooth surface, right side down. Use masking tape to fasten the corners and sides of the fabric to the surface.

Smooth out the batting over the backing. If it is very wrinkled, let it relax overnight before you layer the quilt. Lay the quilt top, right side up, on the batting. Pin the three layers together in several places.

Using a long needle and light-colored thread, begin basting in the center and baste a large X through the center of the quilt layers. Then add parallel rows of basting, spaced 4" to 6" apart. The more rows of basting you have, the better your layers will stay together. Baste around the outer raw edges of the quilt top.

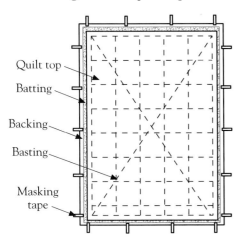

Quilting

Quilting stitches hold the layers of the quilt together. The quilt top, batting, and backing become one when the small running stitches are added. Quilting stitches can be straight lines that follow the lines of patchwork in the quilt, they can outline appliqué designs, or they can embellish spaces between the designs.

QUILTING SUPPLIES

Quilting needles, also called "Betweens," are short needles made especially for quilting. They come in sizes 7, 8, 9, 10, and 12, the larger numbers being the thinner, smaller needles. If you are a beginning quilter, start with size 8 to get used to the shortness of the needle, then work your way down to a smaller size. Purchase a package of assorted sizes and experiment to see which size works best for you. With thinner needles and a little practice, your stitches will get smaller.

Look for the words "quilting thread" on the spool when you buy thread to quilt your project. Quilting thread is thicker than all-purpose thread. It comes in all-cotton and cotton-polyester blends. Some quilting threads are waxed to help prevent tangling. Many quilters choose white or off-white quilting thread to blend with the fabrics in their quilts.

When quilting, be sure to use a thimble to protect your finger and help push the needle through the layers of fabric and batting. Thimbles are usually worn on the middle finger of your sewing hand. A metal thimble with a ridge along the top edge will help guide the needle through the fabric as it pushes the blunt end of the needle. Leather thimbles are soft and will help you become accustomed to wearing a thimble if a metal one seems too cumbersome. Some quilters wear a thimble on the hand below the quilt when quilting on a frame or hoop. This protects their finger from the point of the needle as it pierces the quilt.

THE QUILTING STITCH

Quilting stitches are short running stitches used to sew the top, batting, and backing of your quilt together.

1. To begin quilting, tie a single knot in the end of an 18" length of quilting thread. Start to quilt by inserting the needle through the top layer of the quilt about 3/4" away from the point where you want to start stitching. Slide the needle through the batting layer and bring the needle out at the starting point.

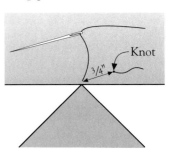

2. Gently tug on the thread until the knot pops through the fabric and is buried in the batting. Take a backstitch and begin quilting, making a small running stitch that goes through all layers. Take two, three, or four stitches at a time, trying to keep them straight and even.

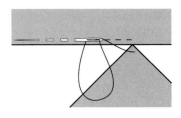

3. When you end your quilting stitches, make a single knot approximately 1/4" from your quilt top. Take one more backstitch into your quilt, tugging the knot into the batting layer and bringing the needle out 3/4" away from your stitches. Clip the thread and let the end disappear into your quilt.

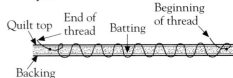

Binding

Binding adds the finishing touch to your quilt. It is usually a good idea to use a darker fabric to frame your design.

1. If you have not already done so, baste around the outer edge of your quilt to securely hold the three layers together. Trim any excess threads, batting, and backing even with the quilt-top edges.

2. Measure the distance around your quilt and add 10". You will need this length of binding to finish your quilt. Cutting across the fabric width, cut enough 2"-wide strips of binding fabric to piece the desired length. Use a rotary cutter, ruler, and mat to do this quickly and accurately.

3. Sew the strips together, using diagonal seams, to create one long strip of binding. To make diagonal seams the easy way, cross two strip ends at right angles, right sides together. Lay these on a flat surface and imagine the strips as a large letter "A." Draw a line across the crossed pieces to "cross the A," then sew along the line. Your seam will be exact, and you can unfold a continuous strip. Trim away the excess fabric, leaving a 1/4"-wide seam allowance. Press this seam open to distribute the thickness of the seam.

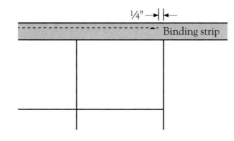

4. Fold the binding strip in half lengthwise, wrong sides together, and press with a hot steam iron.

5. Align the two cut edges of the binding strip with the front cut edge of the quilt. Start sewing the strip approximately 6" from one of the corners, using a 1/4"-wide seam. For durability, sew this seam by machine.

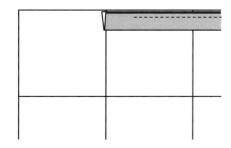

6. To miter the corners of the binding, stop stitching 1/4" from the corner and backstitch.

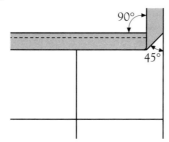

7. Fold the binding diagonally as shown so that it extends straight up from the second edge of the quilt.

8. Then, fold the binding down even with the second edge of the quilt. The fold should be even with the

first edge. Start sewing the binding 1/4" from the fold, making sure to backstitch.

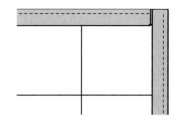

9. To connect the ends of the binding, allow the end to overlap the beginning edge by 2". Cut the end diagonally, with the shortest end of the diagonal on top, nearest to you. Turn the diagonal edge under 1/4" and insert the beginning "tail" inside the diagonal fold.

Turn under 1/4" on diagonal end.

Tuck end inside.

10. Complete the stitching at the join.

11. Fold the binding over the edge of the quilt. The folded edge of the binding should cover the stitching on the back of the quilt. Fold one side first, then the other, to create a miter at each corner. Hand stitch the binding to the back of the quilt, using the traditional appliqué stitch.

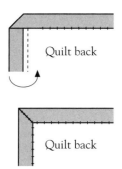

Adding a Label

Very little information is known about many of the quilts in the collection of the Smithsonian Institution. We would love to know more about the quiltmakers and their lives. We have learned from the quilters who have come before us that it is important to identify our work. This gives important information to future quiltmakers and quilt lovers. Here is a label that you can trace for your own special quilt.

1. Photocopy the label so that you can practice writing your quiltmaker's information in the space. Include your name, your address, the date, a dedication, or a special story about the quilt.
2. Make a "good copy" with all the information written in place on the label.
3. Tape the copy to a light box or source of light that will shine through the copy.
4. Cut a piece of plain fabric 1" larger than the label. Iron a piece of freezer paper to the wrong side of the fabric to stabilize it while you write.
5. Tape the fabric over the label copy.
6. Use a fine-line permanent marker (Pigma™ pen) to trace the label design and your information on the fabric. Remove the freezer paper.
7. Sew the label to the back side of your quilt.

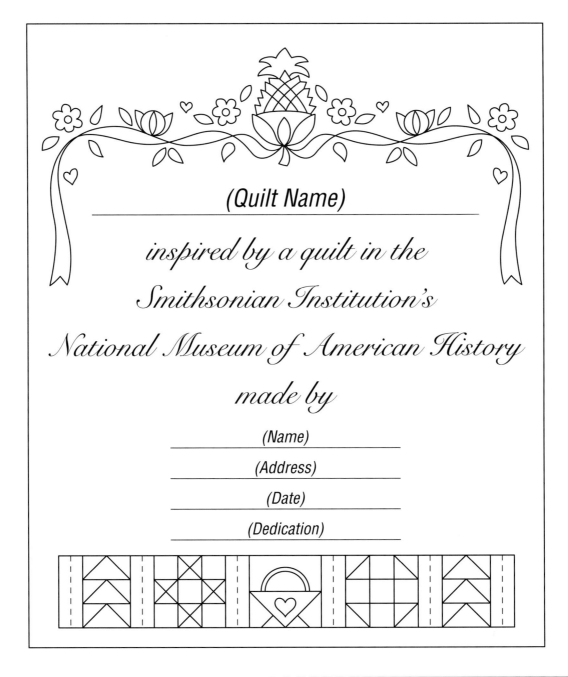

(Quilt Name)

inspired by a quilt in the

Smithsonian Institution's

National Museum of American History

made by

(Name)

(Address)

(Date)

(Dedication)

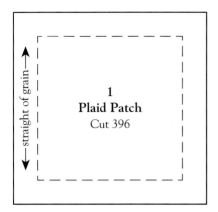

1
Plaid Patch
Cut 396

straight of grain

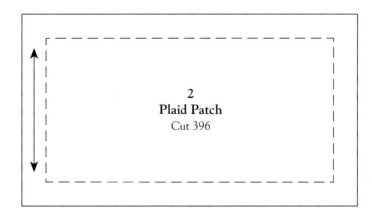

2
Plaid Patch
Cut 396

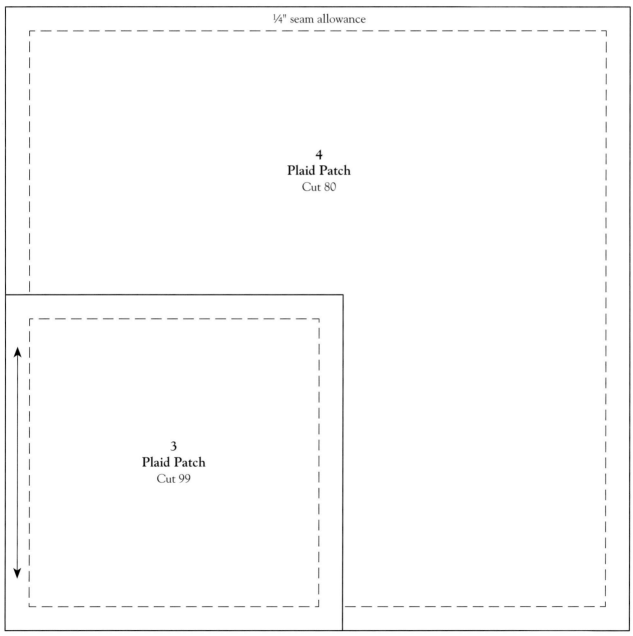

¼" seam allowance

4
Plaid Patch
Cut 80

3
Plaid Patch
Cut 99

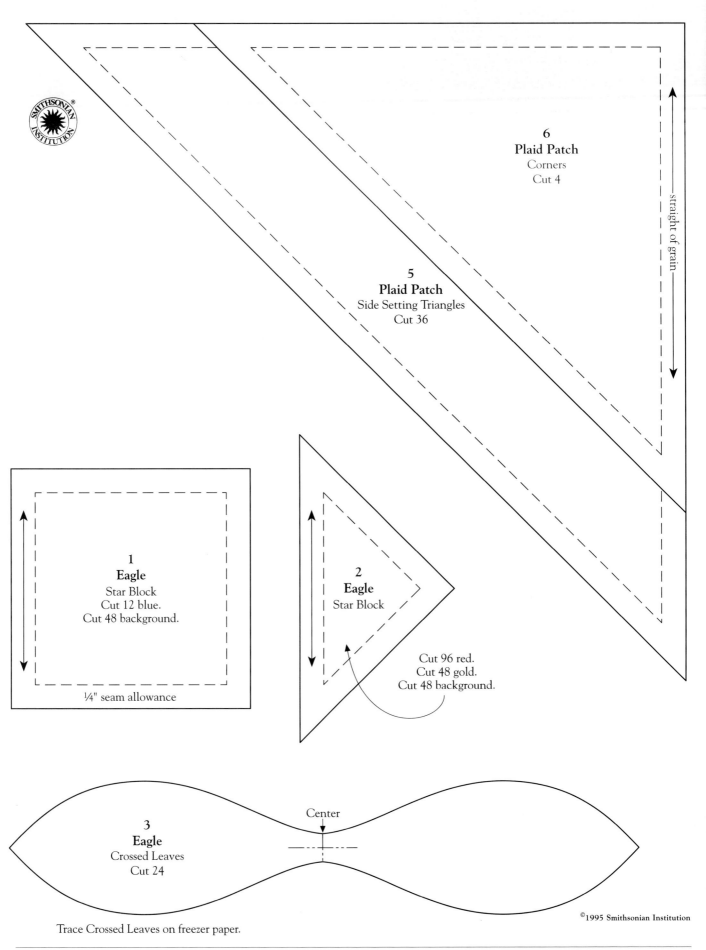

6
Plaid Patch
Corners
Cut 4

straight of grain

5
Plaid Patch
Side Setting Triangles
Cut 36

1
Eagle
Star Block
Cut 12 blue.
Cut 48 background.

¼" seam allowance

2
Eagle
Star Block

Cut 96 red.
Cut 48 gold.
Cut 48 background.

Center

3
Eagle
Crossed Leaves
Cut 24

Trace Crossed Leaves on freezer paper.

©1995 Smithsonian Institution

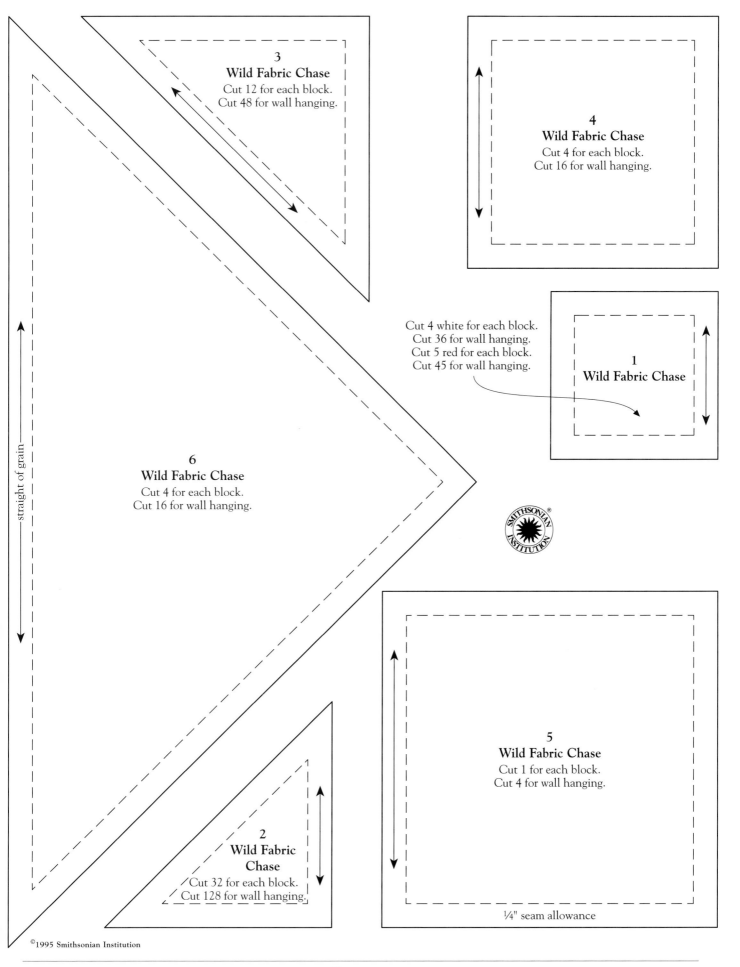

3
Wild Fabric Chase
Cut 12 for each block.
Cut 48 for wall hanging.

4
Wild Fabric Chase
Cut 4 for each block.
Cut 16 for wall hanging.

Cut 4 white for each block.
Cut 36 for wall hanging.
Cut 5 red for each block.
Cut 45 for wall hanging.

1
Wild Fabric Chase

straight of grain

6
Wild Fabric Chase
Cut 4 for each block.
Cut 16 for wall hanging.

5
Wild Fabric Chase
Cut 1 for each block.
Cut 4 for wall hanging.

2
**Wild Fabric
Chase**
Cut 32 for each block.
Cut 128 for wall hanging.

¼" seam allowance

©1995 Smithsonian Institution

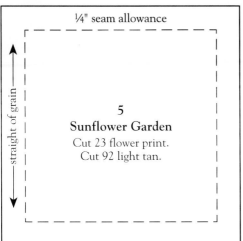

¼" seam allowance

straight of grain

5
Sunflower Garden
Cut 23 flower print.
Cut 92 light tan.

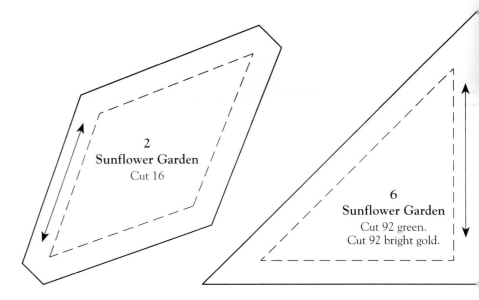

2
Sunflower Garden
Cut 16

6
Sunflower Garden
Cut 92 green.
Cut 92 bright gold.

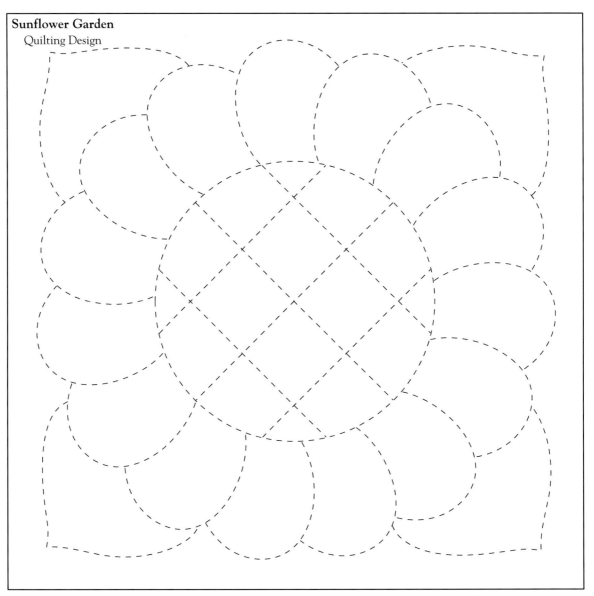

Sunflower Garden
Quilting Design

©1995 Smithsonian Institution

    ✌ TEMPLATES ✌

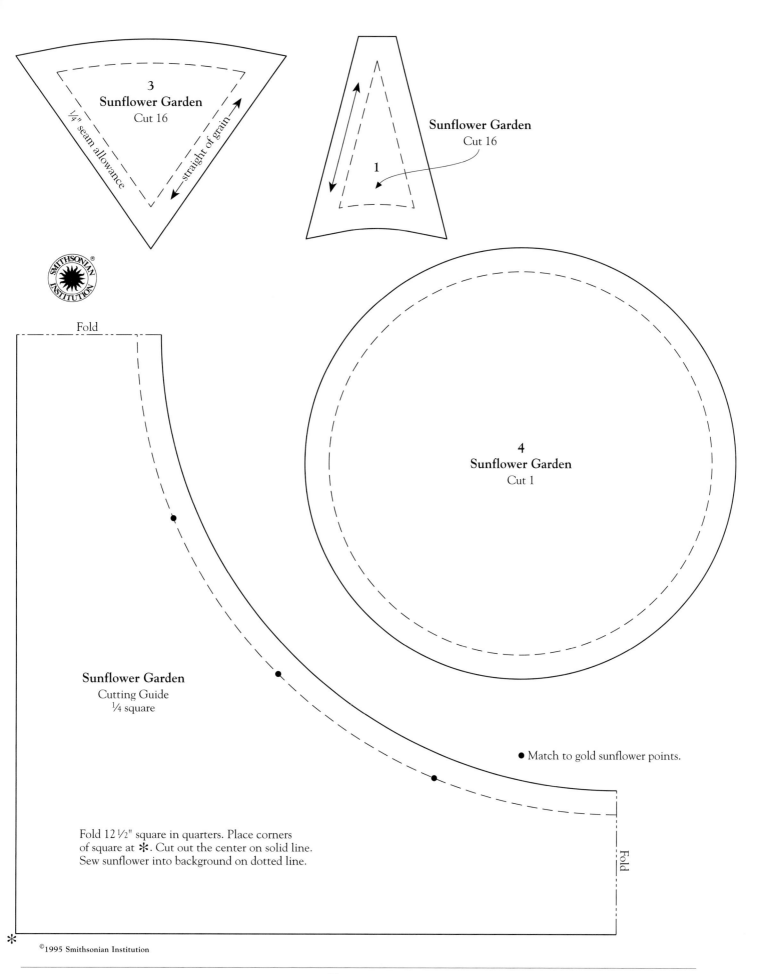

3
Sunflower Garden
Cut 16

¼" seam allowance

straight of grain

Sunflower Garden
Cut 16

1

4
Sunflower Garden
Cut 1

Fold

Sunflower Garden
Cutting Guide
¼ square

● Match to gold sunflower points.

Fold

Fold 12 ½" square in quarters. Place corners
of square at ✳. Cut out the center on solid line.
Sew sunflower into background on dotted line.

✳

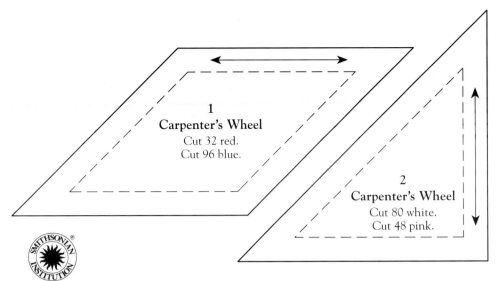

1
Carpenter's Wheel
Cut 32 red.
Cut 96 blue.

2
Carpenter's Wheel
Cut 80 white.
Cut 48 pink.

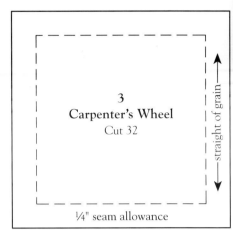

3
Carpenter's Wheel
Cut 32

— straight of grain —

¼" seam allowance

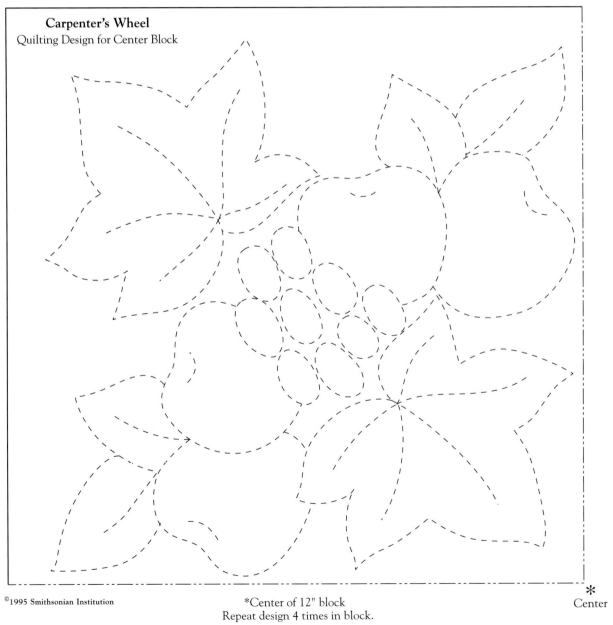

Carpenter's Wheel
Quilting Design for Center Block

*Center of 12" block
Repeat design 4 times in block.

✱
Center

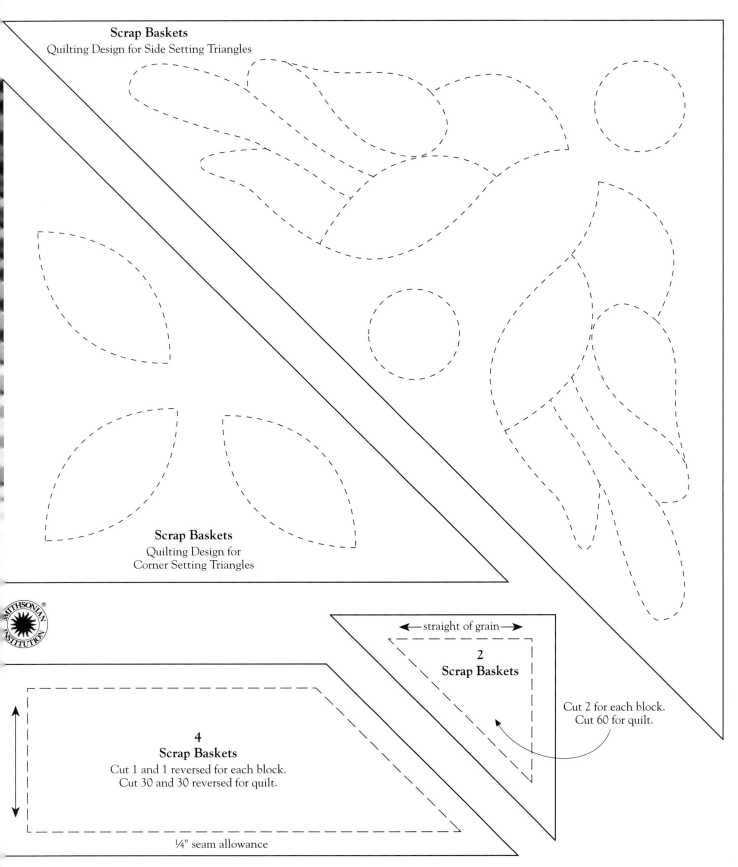

Scrap Baskets
Quilting Design for Side Setting Triangles

Scrap Baskets
Quilting Design for
Corner Setting Triangles

←—— straight of grain ——→

2
Scrap Baskets

Cut 2 for each block.
Cut 60 for quilt.

4
Scrap Baskets
Cut 1 and 1 reversed for each block.
Cut 30 and 30 reversed for quilt.

¼" seam allowance

1995 Smithsonian Institution

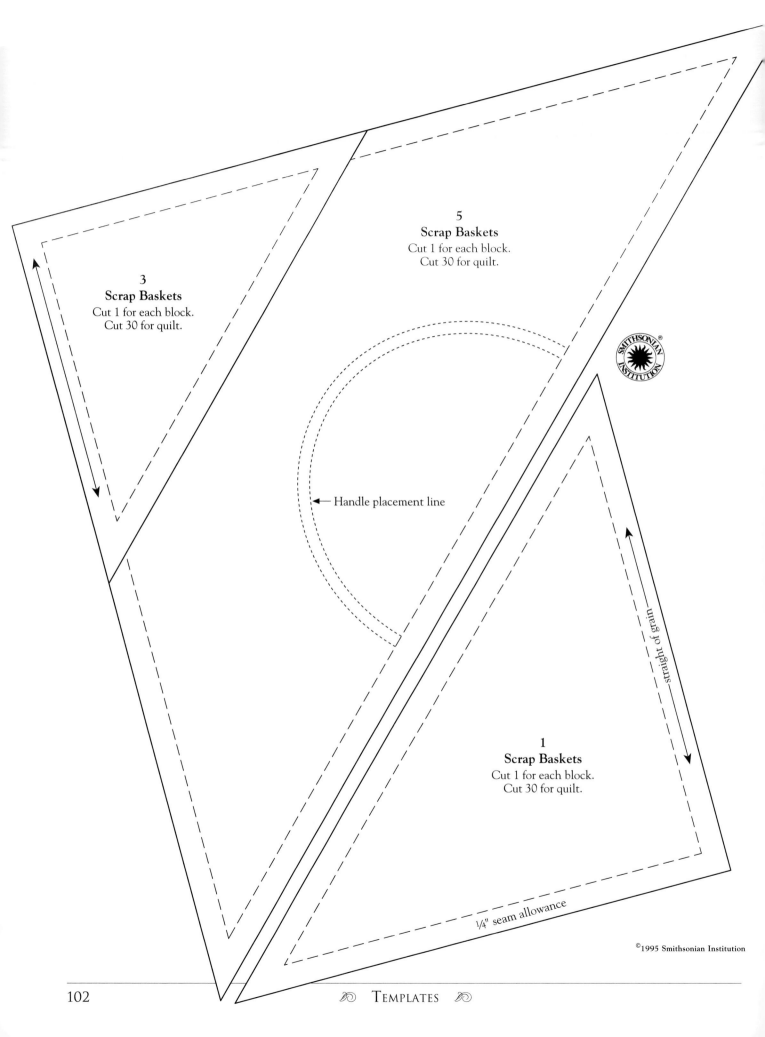

3
Scrap Baskets

Cut 1 for each block.
Cut 30 for quilt.

5
Scrap Baskets

Cut 1 for each block.
Cut 30 for quilt.

← Handle placement line

straight of grain

1
Scrap Baskets

Cut 1 for each block.
Cut 30 for quilt.

¼" seam allowance

Scrap Baskets
Quilting Design
for Setting Block

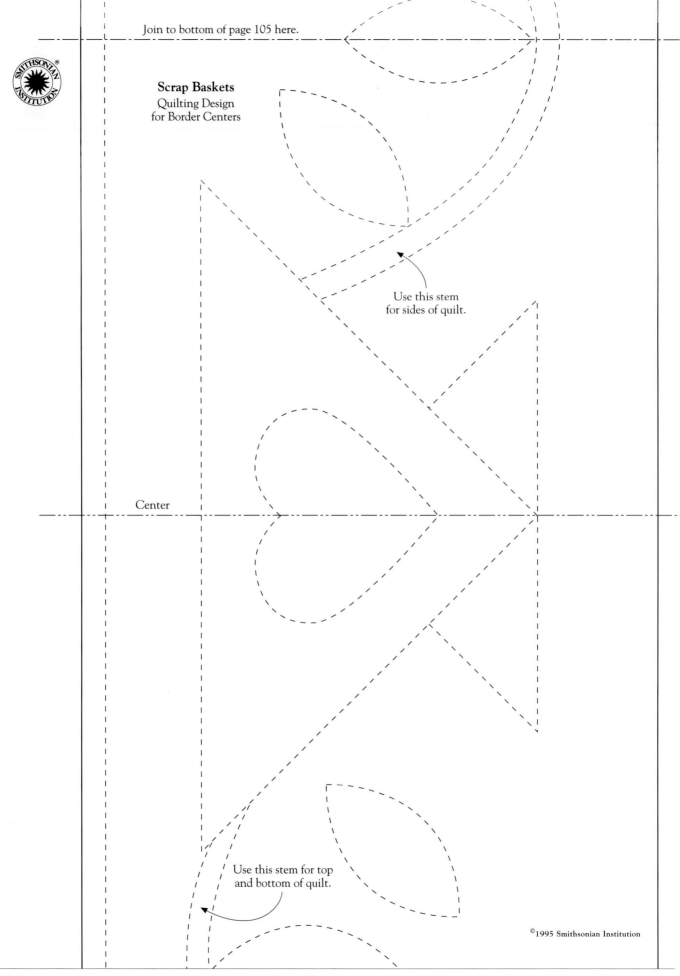

Join to bottom of page 105 here.

Scrap Baskets
Quilting Design
for Border Centers

Use this stem
for sides of quilt.

Center

Use this stem for top
and bottom of quilt.

©1995 Smithsonian Institution

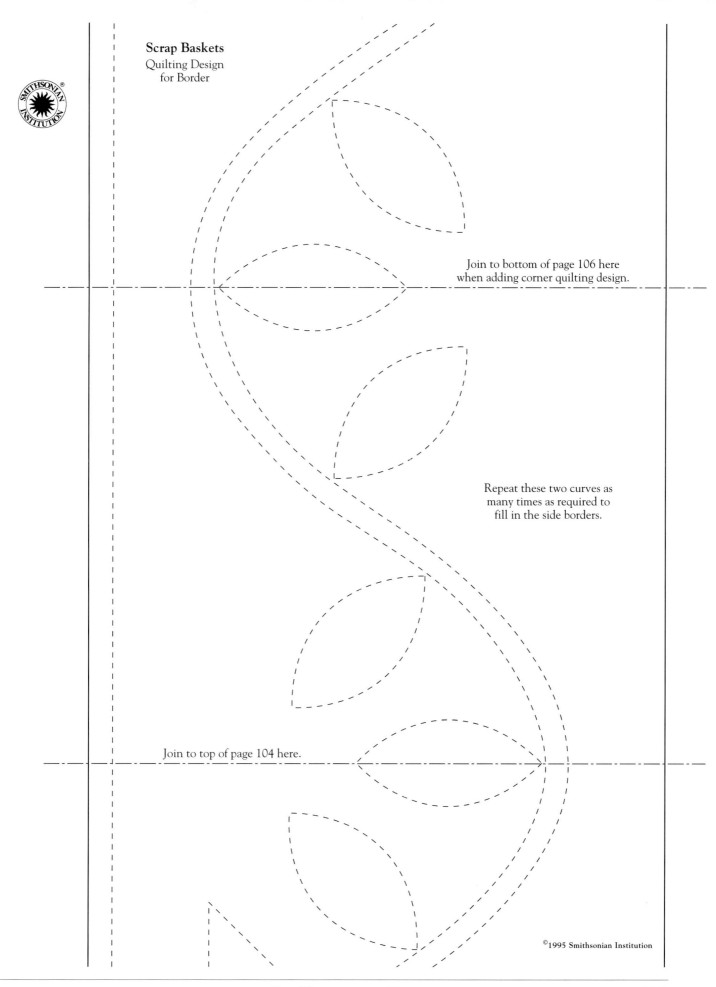

Scrap Baskets
Quilting Design
for Border

Join to bottom of page 106 here
when adding corner quilting design.

Repeat these two curves as
many times as required to
fill in the side borders.

Join to top of page 104 here.

©1995 Smithsonian Institution

Scrap Baskets
Quilting Design
for Border Corners

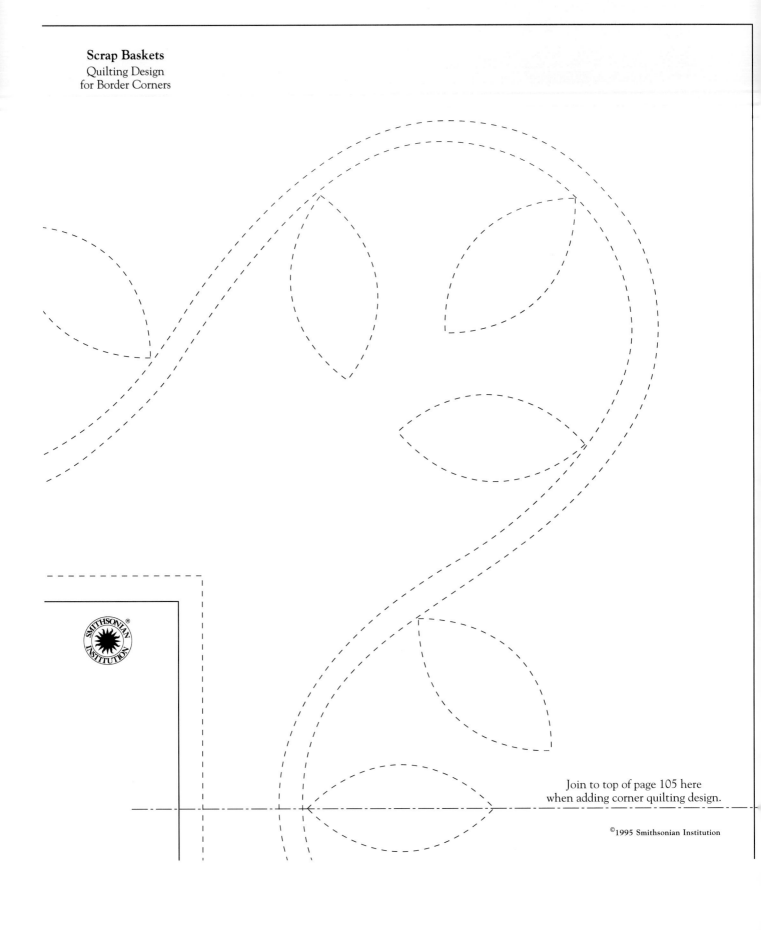

Join to top of page 105 here
when adding corner quilting design.

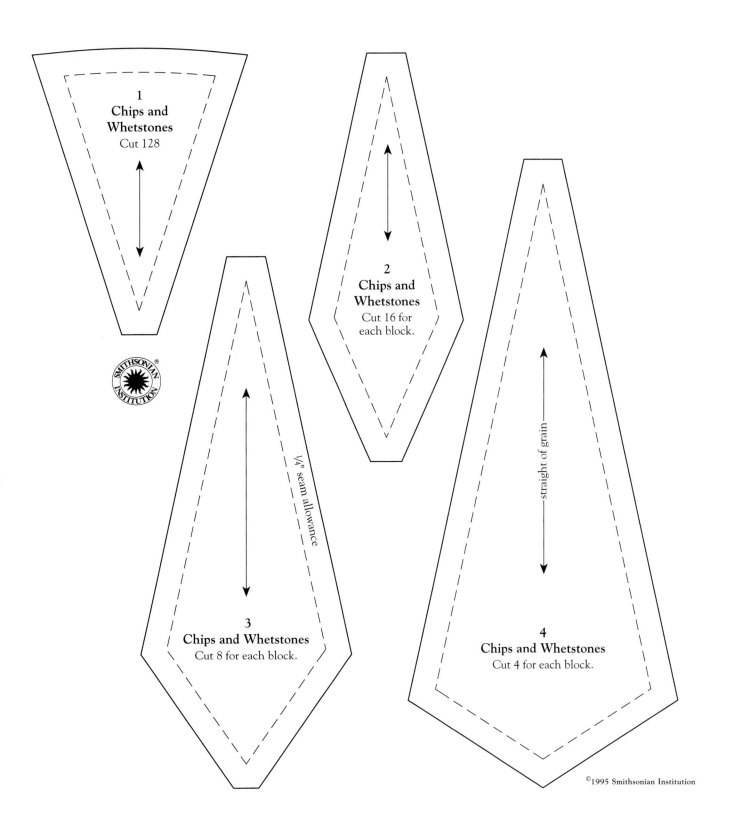

1
Chips and Whetstones
Cut 128

2
Chips and Whetstones
Cut 16 for each block.

3
Chips and Whetstones
Cut 8 for each block.

¼" seam allowance

4
Chips and Whetstones
Cut 4 for each block.

straight of grain

©1995 Smithsonian Institution

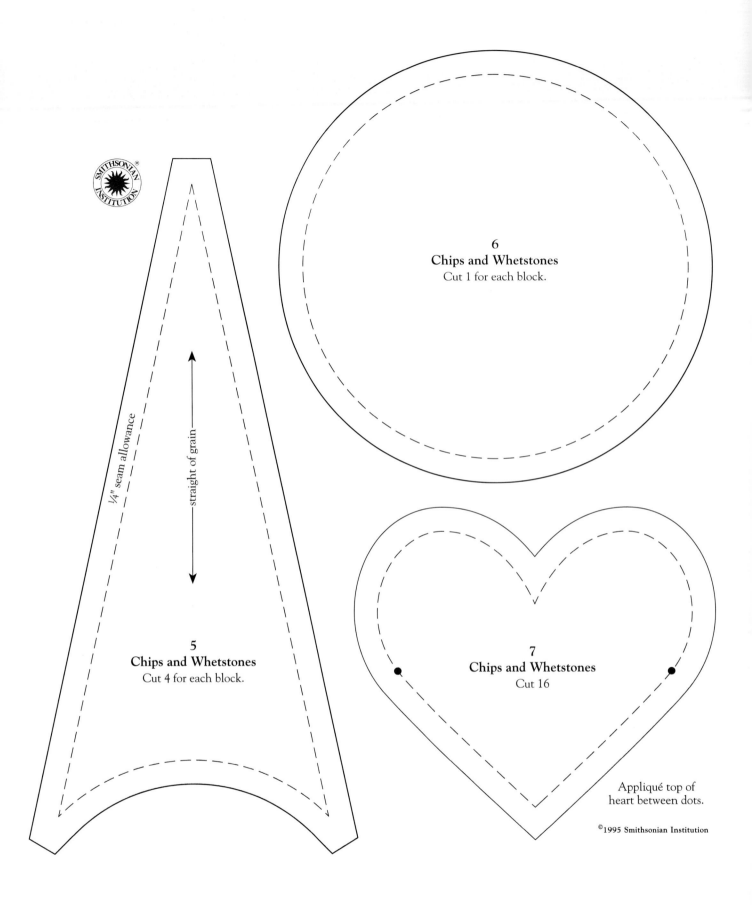

¼" seam allowance

straight of grain

5
Chips and Whetstones
Cut 4 for each block.

6
Chips and Whetstones
Cut 1 for each block.

7
Chips and Whetstones
Cut 16

Appliqué top of
heart between dots.

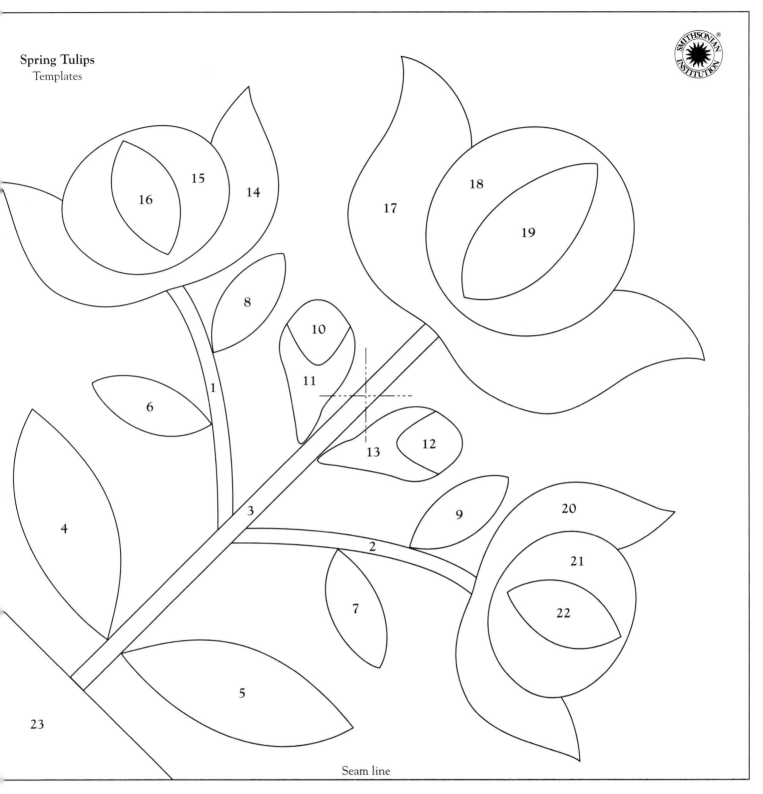

Seam line

Welcome Pineapple
Quilting Design

©1995 Smithsonian Institution

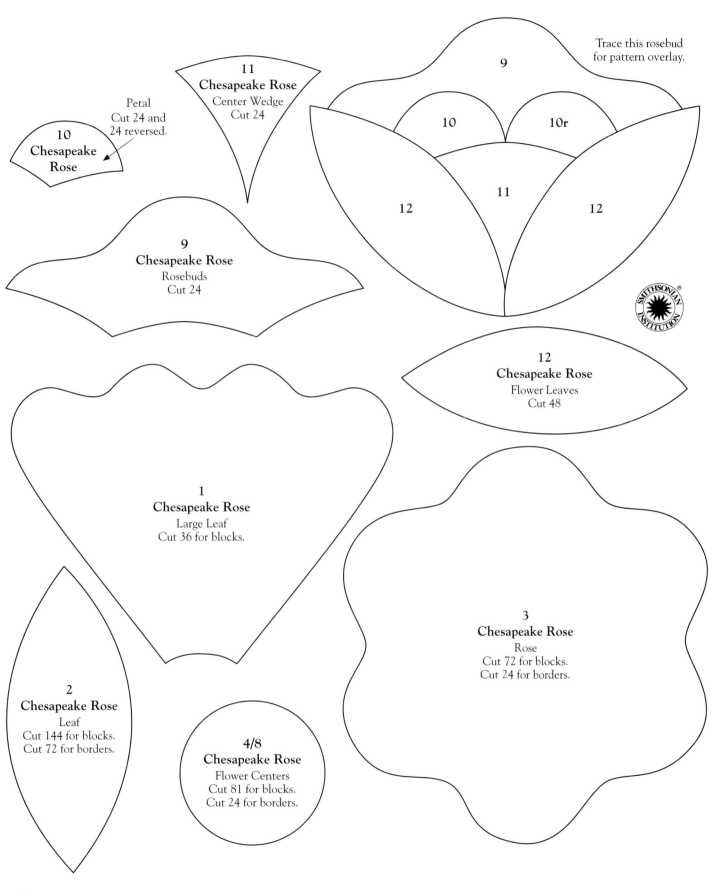

11
Chesapeake Rose
Center Wedge
Cut 24

9

Trace this rosebud
for pattern overlay.

10
9r

11

12
12

Petal
Cut 24 and
24 reversed.

10
**Chesapeake
Rose**

9
Chesapeake Rose
Rosebuds
Cut 24

12
Chesapeake Rose
Flower Leaves
Cut 48

1
Chesapeake Rose
Large Leaf
Cut 36 for blocks.

3
Chesapeake Rose
Rose
Cut 72 for blocks.
Cut 24 for borders.

2
Chesapeake Rose
Leaf
Cut 144 for blocks.
Cut 72 for borders.

4/8
Chesapeake Rose
Flower Centers
Cut 81 for blocks.
Cut 24 for borders.

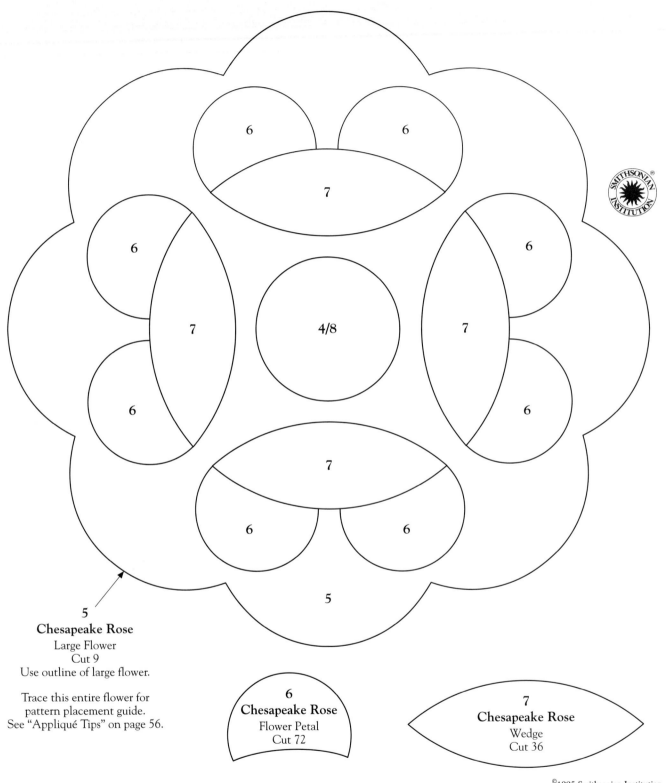

5
Chesapeake Rose
Large Flower
Cut 9
Use outline of large flower.

Trace this entire flower for
pattern placement guide.
See "Appliqué Tips" on page 56.

6
Chesapeake Rose
Flower Petal
Cut 72

7
Chesapeake Rose
Wedge
Cut 36

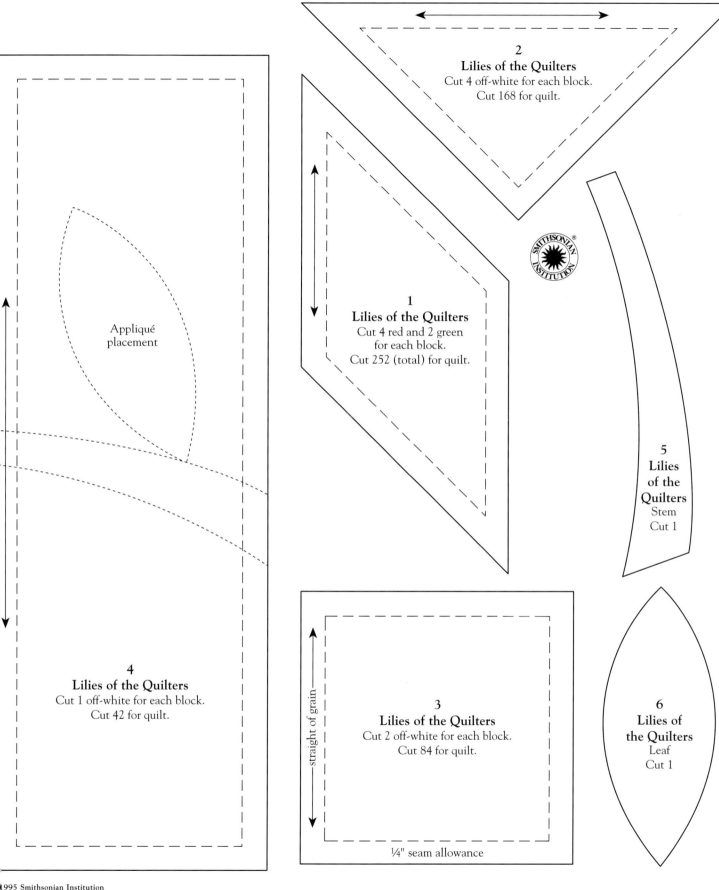

2
Lilies of the Quilters
Cut 4 off-white for each block.
Cut 168 for quilt.

1
Lilies of the Quilters
Cut 4 red and 2 green
for each block.
Cut 252 (total) for quilt.

Appliqué
placement

4
Lilies of the Quilters
Cut 1 off-white for each block.
Cut 42 for quilt.

5
**Lilies
of the
Quilters**
Stem
Cut 1

3
Lilies of the Quilters
Cut 2 off-white for each block.
Cut 84 for quilt.

straight of grain

¼" seam allowance

6
**Lilies of
the Quilters**
Leaf
Cut 1

Lilies of the Quilters
Quilting Design

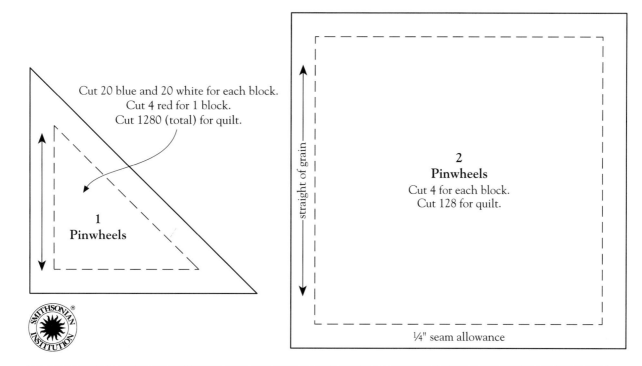

Cut 20 blue and 20 white for each block.
Cut 4 red for 1 block.
Cut 1280 (total) for quilt.

1
Pinwheels

straight of grain

2
Pinwheels
Cut 4 for each block.
Cut 128 for quilt.

¼" seam allowance

Pinwheels
Quilting Designs

Pinwheels
Quilting Design

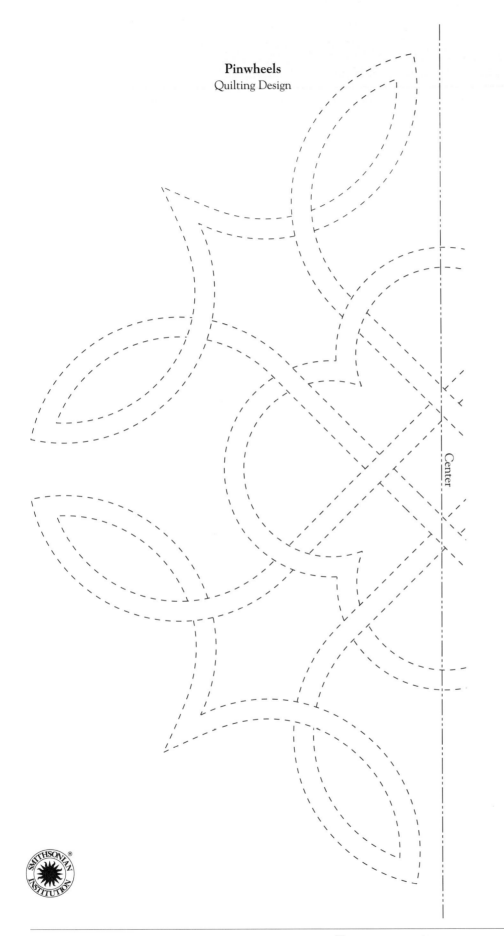

Center

Although this quilting design appears symmetrical, it is not. To make a full-size pattern, trace the pattern given here onto a large piece of paper. Then rotate the tracing 180°, align the center marks, and trace the remaining half.

Trace design

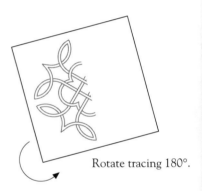

Rotate tracing 180°.

Tracing rotated 180°.

Completed tracing

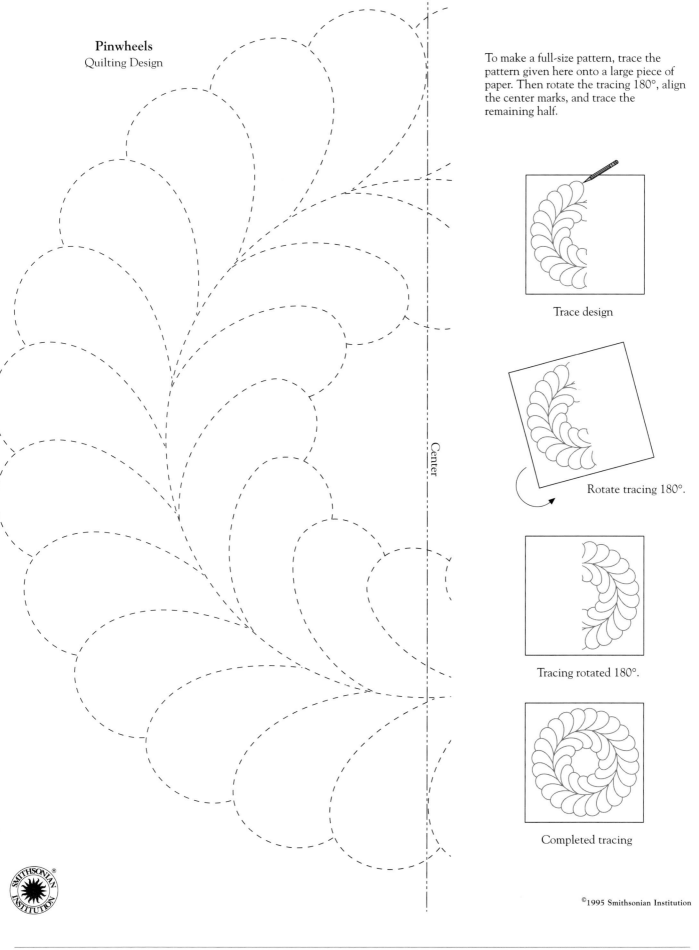

Pinwheels
Quilting Design

To make a full-size pattern, trace the pattern given here onto a large piece of paper. Then rotate the tracing 180°, align the center marks, and trace the remaining half.

Center

Trace design

Rotate tracing 180°.

Tracing rotated 180°.

Completed tracing

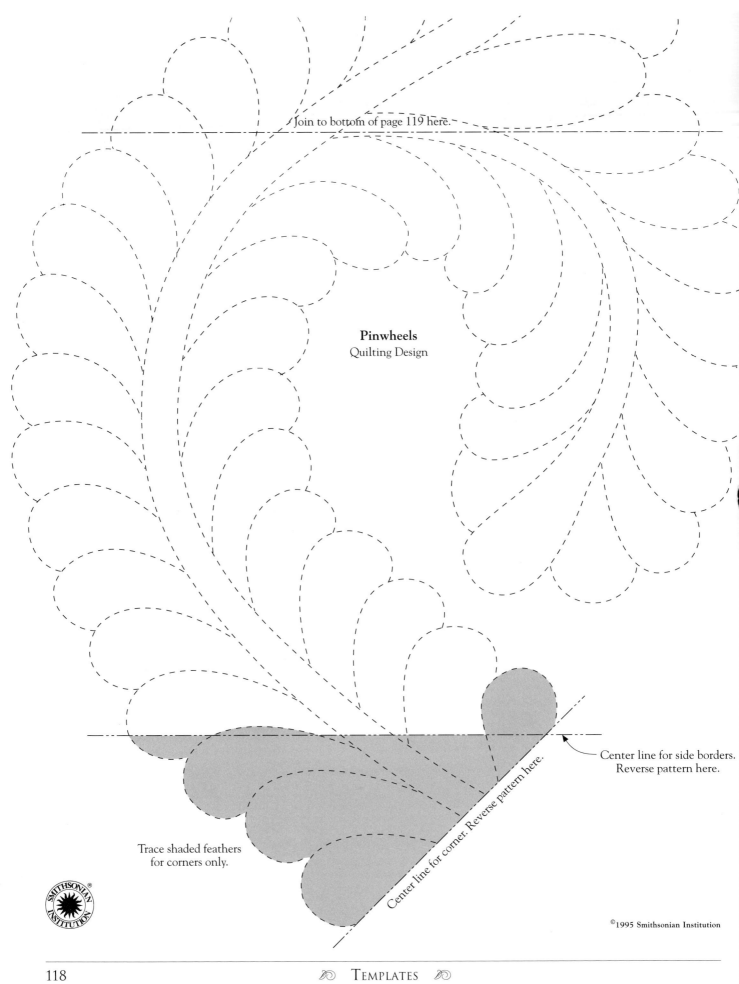

Join to bottom of page 119 here.

Pinwheels
Quilting Design

Center line for side borders.
Reverse pattern here.

Center line for corner. Reverse pattern here.

Trace shaded feathers
for corners only.

©1995 Smithsonian Institution

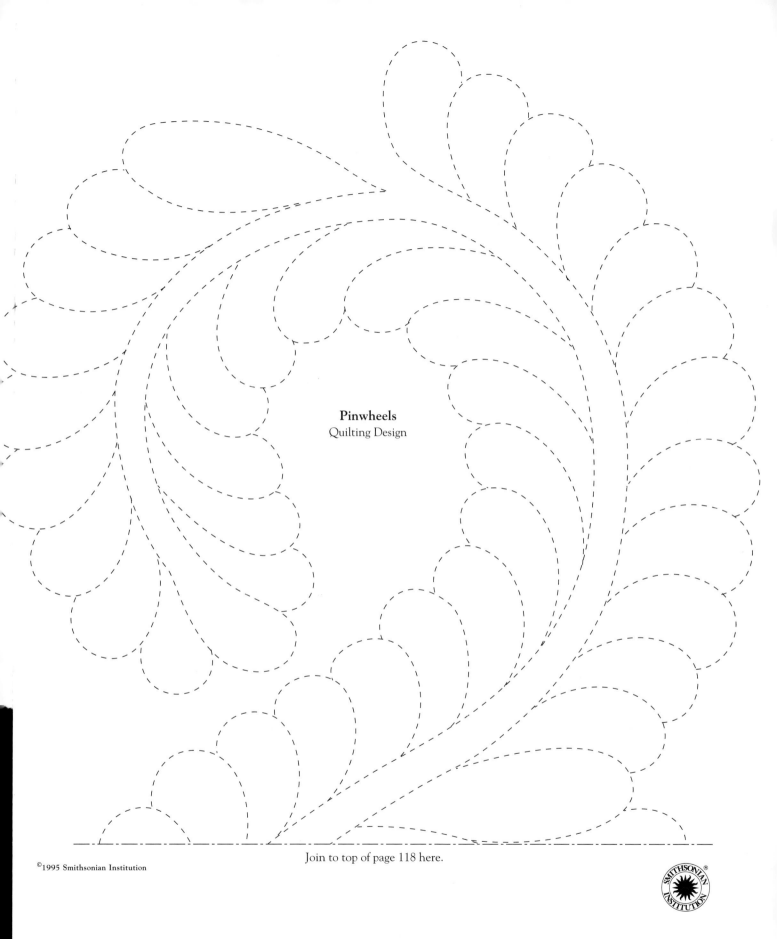

Pinwheels
Quilting Design

Join to top of page 118 here.

That Patchwork Place Publications and Products

All the Blocks Are Geese by Mary Sue Suit
All New Copy Art for Quilters
All-Star Sampler by Roxanne Carter
Angle Antics by Mary Hickey
Animas Quilts by Jackie Robinson
Appliqué Borders: An Added Grace
    by Jeana Kimball
Appliqué in Bloom by Gabrielle Swain
Appliquilt™ for Christmas by Tonee White
Appliquilt™: Whimsical One-Step Appliqué
    by Tonee White
Appliquilt™ Your ABCs by Tonee White
Around the Block with Judy Hopkins
Baltimore Bouquets by Mimi Dietrich
Bargello Quilts by Marge Edie
Basic Beauties by Eileen Westfall
Bias Square® Miniatures
    by Christine Carlson
Biblical Blocks by Rosemary Makhan
Blockbender Quilts by Margaret J. Miller
Block by Block by Beth Donaldson
Borders by Design by Paulette Peters
Botanical Wreaths by Laura M. Reinstatler
The Calico House by Joanna Brazier
The Cat's Meow by Janet Kime
A Child's Garden of Quilts
    by Christal Carter
Colourwash Quilts by Deirdre Amsden
Corners in the Cabin by Paulette Peters
Country Medallion Sampler by Carol Doak
Country Threads by Connie Tesene and
    Mary Tendall
Decoupage Quilts by Barbara Roberts
Designing Quilts by Suzanne Hammond
The Easy Art of Appliqué
    by Mimi Dietrich & Roxi Eppler
Easy Machine Paper Piecing by Carol Doak
Easy Mix & Match Machine Paper Piecing
    by Carol Doak
Easy Paper-Pieced Keepsake Quilts
    by Carol Doak
Easy Quilts...By Jupiter!®
    by Mary Beth Maison
Easy Reversible Vests by Carol Doak
Fantasy Flowers
    by Doreen Cronkite Burbank
Five- and Seven-Patch Blocks & Quilts
    for the ScrapSaver by Judy Hopkins
Four-Patch Blocks & Quilts for the
    ScrapSaver by Judy Hopkins
Freedom in Design by Mia Rozmyn
Fun with Fat Quarters by Nancy J. Martin
Go Wild with Quilts by Margaret Rolfe
Great Expectations by Karey Bresenhan
Happy Endings by Mimi Dietrich
The Heirloom Quilt by Yolande Filson
    and Roberta Przybylski

In The Beginning by Sharon Evans Yenter
Irma's Sampler by Irma Eskes
Jacket Jazz by Judy Murrah
Jacket Jazz Encore by Judy Murrah
The Joy of Quilting by Joan Hanson and
    Mary Hickey
Le Rouvray by Diane de Obaldia,
    with Marie-Christine Flocard
    and Cosabeth Parriaud
Little Quilts by Alice Berg, Sylvia Johnson,
    and Mary Ellen Von Holt
Lively Little Logs by Donna McConnell
Loving Stitches by Jeana Kimball
Machine Quilting Made Easy
    by Maurine Noble
Make Room for Quilts by Nancy J. Martin
Nifty Ninepatches by Carolann M. Palmer
Nine-Patch Blocks & Quilts for the
    ScrapSaver by Judy Hopkins
Not Just Quilts by Jo Parrott
Oh! Christmas Trees
    compiled by Barbara Weiland
On to Square Two by Marsha McCloskey
Osage County Quilt Factory
    by Virginia Robertson
Our Pieceful Village by Lynn Rice
Patchwork Basics by Marie-Christine
    Flocard & Cosabeth Parriaud
A Perfect Match by Donna Lynn Thomas
Picture Perfect Patchwork
    by Naomi Norman
Piecemakers® Country Store
    by the Piecemakers
A Pioneer Doll and Her Quilts
    by Mary Hickey
Pioneer Storybook Quilts by Mary Hickey
Prairie People—Cloth Dolls to Make
    and Cherish by Marji Hadley and
    J. Dianne Ridgley
Quick & Easy Quiltmaking by Mary Hickey,
    Nancy J. Martin, Marsha McCloskey
    and Sara Nephew
The Quilt Patch by Leslie Anne Pfeifer
The Quilt Room by Pam Lintott and
    Rosemary Miller
The Quilted Apple by Laurene Sinema
Quilted for Christmas
    compiled by Ursula Reikes
Quilted for Christmas, Book II
    compiled by Christine Barnes and
    Barbara Weiland
Quilted Sea Tapestries by Ginny Eckley
The Quilters' Companion
    compiled by That Patchwork Place
The Quilting Bee
    by Jackie Wolff and Lori Aluna
Quilting Makes the Quilt by Lee Cleland

Quilts for All Seasons by Christal Carter
Quilts for Baby: Easy as A, B, C
    by Ursula Reikes
Quilts for Kids by Carolann M. Palmer
Quilts from Nature by Joan Colvin
Quilts from the Smithsonian
    by Mimi Dietrich
Quilts to Share by Janet Kime
Rotary Riot
    by Judy Hopkins and Nancy J. Martin
Rotary Roundup
    by Judy Hopkins and Nancy J. Martin
Round About Quilts by J. Michelle Watts
Round Robin Quilts
    by Pat Magaret and Donna Slusser
Samplings from the Sea
    by Rosemary Makhan
ScrapMania by Sally Schneider
Seasoned with Quilts by Retta Warehime
Sensational Settings by Joan Hanson
Sewing on the Line
    by Lesly-Claire Greenberg
Shortcuts: A Concise Guide to Rotary
    Cutting by Donna Lynn Thomas
Shortcuts Sampler by Roxanne Carter
Shortcuts to the Top
    by Donna Lynn Thomas
Small Talk by Donna Lynn Thomas
Smoothstitch® Quilts by Roxi Eppler
The Stitchin' Post
    by Jean Wells and Lawry Thorn
Stringing Along by Trice Boerens
Stripples by Donna Lynn Thomas
Sunbonnet Sue All Through the Year
    by Sue Linker
Tea Party Time by Nancy J. Martin
Template-Free® Quiltmaking
    by Trudie Hughes
Template-Free® Quilts and Borders
    by Trudie Hughes
Template-Free® Stars by Jo Parrott
Through the Window & Beyond
    by Lynne Edwards
Treasures from Yesteryear, Book One
    by Sharon Newman
Treasures from Yesteryear, Book Two
    by Sharon Newman
Trouble Free Triangles by Gayle Bong
Two for Your Money by Jo Parrott
Watercolor Impressions by Pat Magaret
    and Donna Slusser
Watercolor Quilts
    by Pat Magaret and Donna Slusser
Woven & Quilted by Mary Anne Caplinger
WOW! Wool-on-Wool Folk Art Quilts
    by Janet Carija Brandt

4", 6", 8", & metric Bias Square® • BiRangle™ • Ruby Beholder™ • ScrapMaster • Rotary Rule™ • Rotary Mate™
Shortcuts to America's Best-Loved Quilts (video)

Many titles are available at your local quilt shop. For more information, send $2 for a color catalog to
That Patchwork Place, Inc., PO Box 118, Bothell WA 98041-0118 USA.

☎ Call 1-800-426-3126 for the name and location of the quilt shop nearest you.